PROBLEM RESOLUTION

EFFECTIVENESS AND EFFICIENCY

DISCIPLINE AND METHODOLOGIES

and the ROLE of

ARTIFICIAL INTELLIGENCE

By

HARRY K. JAMES

PGH PRESS

Published by PGH Press
www.linkedin.com/in/harryjames

Ordering Information
Quantity sales: Special discounts are available on quantity purchases by corporations, associations, and others. For details, contact the publisher at the address above.
Publisher's Cataloging-in-Publication Data
Names: James, Harry, author.
Title: Problem Resolution Effectiveness and Efficiency Discipline and Methodologies and the Role of Artificial Intelligence
Description: First edition. | PGH Press, 2026. | Includes bibliographical references and index.
Identifiers:
ISBN: 979-8-9962626-1-8 (Paperback)
ISBN: 979-8-9962626-2-5 (Hardcover)
ISBN: 979-8-9962626-0-1 (eBook)
Subjects: BISAC: BUSINESS & ECONOMICS / Decision Making % Problem Solving | BUSINESS & ECONOMICS./ Management. | COMPUTERS / Artificial Intelligence / General. | TECHNOLOGY & ENGINEERING / General.

AI Disclosure & Technical Disclaimer
Portions of the case studies and data analyses in this work were demonstrated using Artificial Intelligence (AI) assistants. All AI-generated outputs, analyses, and solutions were meticulously audited, reviewed, and validated by the author to ensure technical accuracy and adherence to the 8D and Fishbone methodologies.

Printed in the United States of America

For

Erik
Annie
Jack

and

Edwin Alexander, M.D.
and
Shauna Aiello

Problem Resolution

Table of Contents

PROLOGUE

This book is meant to present retrospective examples of resolved problems to demonstrate the use of aids for applying discipline and methodology to resolve problems effectively and efficiently.

There are several historical books that focus on accurately delineating the problem to be resolved but not with examples detailing the formal process documentation, disciplined methodologies and supplemental aids to support the process. None of these books describes the emerging use of artificial intelligence.

Among those books are:

The Rational Manager, A Systematic Approach to Problem Solving and Decision Making by Charles H. Kepner and Benjamin B. Tregoe, Kepner-Tregoe, Inc., 1965, ISBN 10-0070341753

The Proactive Manager, The Complete Book of Problem Solving and Decision Making by Lorne C. Plunkett and Guy A. Hale, John Wiley and Sons, Inc., 1982, ISBN 0-471-08509-X

The IDEAL Problem Solver, A Guide for Improving Thinking, Learning, and Creativity by John D. Bransford and Barry S. Stein, W. H. Freeman and Company, 1984, ISBN 0-7167-1668-2

Strategic Problem Solving: A Step-By-Step Guide to Solve Hard Problems by Mark Hartley, Las Vegas, 2025, ISBN 9798300329617

Solve It! The Mindset and Tools of Smart Problem Solvers by Dietmar Sternad, Las Vegas, 2025, ISBN 978-3-903386-03-7

These books emphasize methodology but provide few detailed real-world demonstrations. There is little discussion of efficiency or the formality of validation.

The document and discipline methodology that has been developed over time is meant to capture the essence and focus of the problem and facilitate its resolution. The application of these techniques is herein applied to retrospectively known, solved problems as examples for how to apply this document and methodology discipline successfully. Using retrospective examples, the disciplined problem analysis methodologies and aids are demonstrated with real-life problems.

There are two parts to this book: Part 1 presents the foundation and demonstration of formal processes and documentation; Part 2 describes the emerging role of artificial intelligence as a resolution resource and demonstrates how to use it.

PART 1

Introduction: includes an essential restatement of the problem resolution structure but adds a top layer for formal documented capture of the process that extends the classic approaches with disciplines to answer the problem questions. Additional aids and techniques for problem analysis are presented for more complex problem analysis.

The next four chapters demonstrate the process using real solved retrospective problems.

Chapter 1: a problem and solution encountered by NASA for an Apollo propulsion issue.

Chapter 2: a problem and solution encountered on the Apollo 13 mission.

Chapter 3: a problem and solution for profitability based on product mix analysis.

Chapter 4: a problem and solution for a semiconductor device reliability issue.

PART 2

The last two chapters introduce Artificial Intelligence and its structure followed by a demonstration using AI to solve a real problem.

Chapter 5: the role of Artificial Intelligence as a resource for efficient problem resolution.

Chapter 6: a problem resolution demonstration using AI.

Except for Chapter 2, the author was personally involved in the problem resolutions described herein, either as a team member or as the principal investigator.

Effectiveness and Efficiency

For any action whose purpose is to achieve a task completion, there are two measures: effectiveness and efficiency. Effectiveness: was the task accomplished? Efficiency: was the task completed with timeliness?

The primary focus of most processes for problem resolution is effectiveness. However, it is universally understood that "time is money". A problem that interrupts a process, results in lost time and cost. The time taken to recover from a process interruption results in unanticipated cost.

As part of the process used for resolution, time duration and resources required are integral to accomplish the task. Furthermore, there is the nature of the problem that results in the need for inductive reasoning or deductive reasoning; that is, symptoms versus objective data. The examples presented here represent instances of both types of problems.

Analytical techniques used to anticipate future design or process failures are not presented here. The technique for this purpose is Failure Mode and Effects Analysis (FMEA): it is an anticipatory response to potential problems. FMEA analyzes for potential failure modes in a design or process. The technique evaluates the severity, occurrence, and detection of each failure mode. The technique prioritizes the most critical failure modes for further analysis. There are many sources for FMEA training.

Pareto Analysis is another technique not within the scope of this book. Pareto analysis attempts to capture and measure the frequency of multiple discrepancies in the performance of a design or process and rank the occurrences according to their frequency to determine on which deficiencies to focus resources for improvement.

Presented here is a demonstrated set of disciplined procedures, tools and methods for specific problem articulation and focus to achieve validated resolution in the shortest time possible.

This presentation also reflects the evolution over time for the rapid change in problem resolution approach as new methodologies, resources and resolution aids, such as Artificial Intelligence have become available to facilitate more efficient resolution. A comparative demonstration of AI's ability to enhance problem resolution comprehensively is provided.

Introduction

Part One

Overview

In any problem, articulation of the problem is the most important action – it creates and assures continuing focus.

It is mandatory to document your resolution process in writing. Verbal discussions can be misinterpreted by the listeners based on normal human biases. A written record is less likely to be misunderstood by the participants or those who requested the problem resolution.

If the Problem Statement changes upon interrogation of the information about the problem, adjust and document, but don't lose sight of the goal.

Problem resolution takes time and time-is-money, and time can be as important as resolving the problem.

Any action/goal is measured by its effectiveness and its efficiency of achievement.

A problem is not resolved until its solution is validated.

Articulating the Problem

To accurately articulate a problem statement, first, understand the problem. Gather and interrogate all relevant information about the issue. Talk to affected parties to understand their perspectives and concerns.

Describe the conditions in which the problem exists. Define the context and identify who is affected by the problem and how.

Describe the Impact of the unexpected deficiencies or consequences of the problem. Quantify the impact, if possible (e.g., cost, time, resources), measurements (rates, time, percentage any numerical measures of performance affected).

Establish the scope of the problem; is there a measure of impact? Establish the type of problem (inductive or deductive: detailed below). State what is included and excluded from the problem statement. An excluded item may later be determined to be important. Recording the item may turn out to have pivotal influence. Archiving it in writing preserves it to prevent it from being lost. Record why it was judged not to be relevant.

Ensure the problem statement is clear and easily understandable. Avoid jargon and complex language. Simplify the language used as much as possible.

Share the initial problem statement with other affected individuals for feedback. If appropriate, hold a meeting (virtual, if necessary) to open an initial review for feedback to further clarify details. Revise the problem statement based on feedback to improve clarity and accuracy.

Always create a written record of the investigation progression that results in the final, accepted problem statement. Include supporting data and evidence to back up the statement in writing. Documenting the effort is beneficial to maintain focus without losing sight of seemingly small bits of information that may have pivotal influence on the determination of root cause. Lessons-learned reviews can be done expediently. You never know what may become important to the problem resolution.

Verbal team discussions can be captured today using voice-to-text software on personal computers or one of many hand-held voice-to-text translation devices that can be uploaded to personal computer for printing. These devices can determine the specific speaker being recorded. Some of these available devices will perform editing function to remove extraneous irrelevant sounds and to correct unrecognized speech phonetic interpretations. Some can format a formal report.

Finally, formulate the problem statement, clarify any ambiguities or inconsistent language and take time to assure the problem statement accurately reflects the problem to be resolved. It is better to take the time to resolve the correct problem than to spend time on an erroneous problem.

You can create a clear, concise, and effective problem statement that provides a solid foundation for finding solutions. If a concerned party reads the problem statement and doesn't understand what it says, it is not good enough. No misunderstandings should exist.

Aids

The 5 Whys

The purpose of the "5 Whys" is to move from problem generalizations to a definitive problem statement from which to proceed to identify root cause. It involves asking the question "Why?" five times (or as many times as necessary) to drill down into the details of a problem to uncover its underlying cause.

This method helps to avoid superficial, "knee jerk" fixes: i.e., to avoid "jumping-to-cause" (a Kepner-Tregoe phrase).

A simple illustrative example of the 5 Whys:

Initial Problem Statement: A machine on the production line has stopped working.

1. Why did the machine stop?
   - The machine stopped because it overheated.

2. Why did the machine overheat?
   - The machine overheated because the cooling fan stopped working.

3. Why did the cooling fan stop working?
   - The cooling fan stopped working because it was not maintained regularly.

4. Why was the cooling fan not maintained regularly?
   - The cooling fan was not maintained regularly because there was no preventive maintenance schedule for it.

5. Why was there no preventive maintenance schedule for the cooling fan?
   - There was no preventive maintenance schedule because the machine's maintenance protocols were outdated.

Root Cause: The root cause is the outdated maintenance protocols, which led to the cooling fan not being maintained and eventually caused the machine to overheat and stop.

The corrective action is therefore to update the machine's protocols and maintenance schedule.

Key Points to Consider:

1. Depth of Analysis: Five iterations of "Why?" is a rule-of-thumb, not an absolute. Sometimes, fewer or more questions may be needed to reach the definitive problem statement.
2. Team Involvement: It's beneficial to involve affected parties in the process, as different perspectives can help identify the root cause more effectively.
3. Document Answers: Always write down each question and answer to keep track of the thought process and ensure clarity.
4. Practical Focus: The "5 Whys" should focus on actionable issues that can be addressed rather than abstract or uncontrollable factors.

The "5 Whys" technique is a fundamental tool in many problem resolution methodologies, including Lean, Six Sigma, and Kaizen, due to its effectiveness in promoting deeper analysis and understanding.

Kepner & Tregoe describes this process as "stair-stepping to the problem statement".

8D Written Documentation

The 8D problem resolution process was developed by Ford Motor Company to address complex recurring production problems, both internally and with its supply chain. The process was formalized in Ford Motor Company, *Team Oriented Problem Solving (TOPS) Manual*, 1987. Ford refers to the current variation of this process as G8D or Global 8D.

An 8D document is a formal record used in quality management. It reflects the "Eight Disciplines" approach to problem resolution, which is a structured methodology designed to identify, correct, and eliminate recurring problems. This documentation technique is used heavily in the military, aerospace and space industries by contractors and suppliers to address quality performance issues when they arise. It is also used in the automotive, manufacturing and services industries where systematic problem resolution is critical.

The 8D problem resolution approach is typically used for complex, recurring, or critical problems that require a structured, team-based approach to identify root causes and implement effective solutions. It's particularly helpful when safety or regulatory concerns arise, when there are significant customer complaints or warranty issues, or when internal rejects, waste, or poor performance occur at unacceptable levels.

Purpose and Benefits:

1. Ensures a comprehensive systematic approach to problem resolution that addresses not just the symptoms but the root causes.

2. Focuses on interim actions to safeguard the affected parties while a permanent solution is being developed.
3. Provides thorough documentation that can be used to capture problem information for future reference and continuous improvement.
4. Encourages teamwork and cross-functional collaboration.

The 8D process is divided into eight disciplines or steps:

D1: Select the Investigator(s)

Depending on the scope of the problem, a team may be necessary. The team may include a principal investigator and support members whose time may only be needed intermittently. Or the team may require significant support from many members with cross-functional skills. As the investigation proceeds the number of team members may be reduced or increased, as progress is made. Identify any cross-functional needs for the problem resolution.

D2: Describe the Problem

While this is a simple statement, it is critical to state the problem correctly and unambiguously. Define the problem in measurable terms. Provide a clear and concise description that includes the "what," "where," "when," "who" and "how big."

D3: Develop Interim Containment Actions

Identify and implement actions to protect the impacted process from the problem until permanent corrective action is in place. Describe the short-term actions taken to mitigate the problem's impact and protect the affected parties.

D4: Determine and Verify Root Causes

Identify all potential causes that could explain why the problem occurred. Verify these causes through data analysis and testing. Determine if additional aids (see AIDS below) are necessary to include all the suggested, potential causes.

D5: Choose and Validate Permanent Corrective Actions

Select and verify actions that will permanently resolve the problem by addressing the root causes.

D6: Implement Permanent Corrective Actions

Implement the chosen corrective actions and confirm their effectiveness. Detail the steps for implementing the corrective actions, including resources required, timelines, and responsibilities.

D7: Prevent Recurrence

Modify the management systems, operating systems, practices, and procedures to prevent recurrence of this and similar problems. Describe the changes in detail.

D8: Recognize Team and Individuals

Acknowledge the collective efforts and contributions of the team. Recognize the success and formalize the completed project. Provide a means of closure.

The modified G8D added a "D0" step in which the seriousness of the problem is assessed and a further assessment in the D4 step to analyze how the problem was not detected sooner to prevent its consequences from becoming serious.

An 8D document is a valuable tool for ensuring problems are thoroughly understood, effectively addressed, and prevented from recurring in the future.

An 8D document can be easily created in Microsoft Word or Excel.

With today's ability for computers and other devices to convert speech to text, this is an advantage in capturing the team's efforts to detail and record actions taken to resolve problems. Some devices can also distinguish between speakers. Editing will likely be required to correct grammatical errors in the spoken words. It is also likely that phonetic spelling of jargon or industry "buzzwords" may not be known to the voice-to-text converter programs and will require editing. This capability can have a significant impact on problem resolution efficiency.

Fishbone (Ishikawa) Diagram

Use this template to identify multiple possible causes of a problem by category. List specific causes under each category branch. This structure helps analyze root causes systematically.

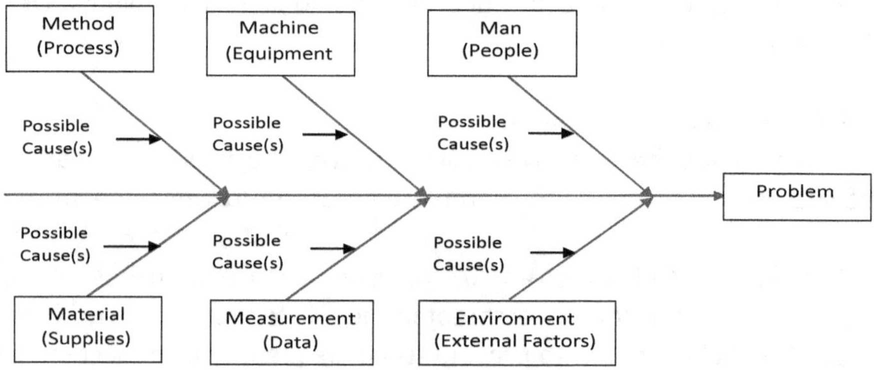

Figure 1: Ishikawa Fishbone Diagram

Identify potential and reasonable causes for each category.

After listing all causes, review them to identify by ranking which may be the most likely root causes to evaluate first. Efficiency in resolution can be as important as determining the effective root cause.

Problem Type: Deductive or Inductive

What Type of Problem is This?

Deductive

A problem that requires deductive logic typically involves measurable conditions, such as numerical quantities, percentages, physical dimensions, etc.

Deductive logic is based on strict logical necessity between premises and conclusions. It is a form of reasoning where conclusions are drawn from a set of premises, and if the premises are true, the conclusion must also be true.

It is a progression that moves from the General-to-Specific. Premises can be objective (e.g., proven scientific laws) or subjective (someone's belief), but the key is that the form of reasoning makes the conclusion necessarily follow if the premises are accepted as true.

Example:
Premise: All cats have four legs. (Could be true or false — question of data.)
Premise: Felix is a cat.
Conclusion: Felix has four legs.

Even if the first premise were wrong, the logical form is deductively valid. Conclusions are certain if the reasoning is valid and the premises are true.

Inductive

A problem that requires inductive logic typically involves subjective symptoms. Inductive logic is based on patterns drawn from observations and evidence, which can be objective or subjective.

Inductive logic involves reasoning from specific observations or cases to broader generalizations or theories. Conclusions are probable, not guaranteed — they can be strong or weak depending on the evidence.

Induction supports forming hypotheses and theories but does not guarantee certainty — it deals with likelihood.

The hypothesis for investigation depends on observed patterns or evidence gathered from specific cases. Observations can be objective (e.g., experimental data) or subjective (e.g., personal experience). Even with objective observations, inductive conclusions are probable, not guaranteed.

Example:
Observation: You observe 100 swans and all are white.
Conclusion: "All swans are white."
But you might later find a black swan — your conclusion was based on a strong but uncertain pattern.

Interrogation of the information describing the elements of the observed and reported deficiency is enough to tell an investigator what type of problem is being faced for resolution.

Validation

Root cause validation is a critical step in the problem resolution process. It ensures that the identified cause is accurate and that subsequent solutions are effective and efficient. It is essential to complete this step. By validating the root cause, organizations or affected parties can prevent the problem from recurring, optimize resource use, and build confidence in investigator(s) problem resolution capabilities.

Validation may not be trivial. Implementing some corrective actions may take significant cost and time.

Validation is complete when the identified root cause corrective action is implemented, and no problem recurrence is observed.

An accurately delineated Problem Statement is only the beginning.

Part Two

Overview

Artificial Intelligence (AI) has emerged to be an important development in popular use by media aficionados. Its use is gaining wide adaptation to information mining and reference searching. It is rapidly displacing reliance on traditional search-engine workflows for many forms of information discovery. It cannot be ignored. It is faster and more comprehensive in scope than anything that preceded it.

Artificial Intelligence is described and its use is demonstrated in comparison to a solution for a retrospective real problem.

Artificial Intelligence

What it is and how It works

AI's influence on information retrieval and analytical workflows is becoming increasingly difficult to ignore. It is faster and more comprehensive in scope than any prior general-purpose information retrieval resource. One cannot uncover reference inquiries as fast as AI can generate them. The focus becomes one of deciding relevance to the problem and can be much more expedient to achieving resolution.

AI's structure is examined. When and how is its database is updated. What differences exist between models. What quality control system is utilized. How can sources be expanded. Where AI is expected to progress in its abilities for good or ill.

Benefits of AI
Speed in accessing supporting information and why it cannot be avoided.

Caveats of AI
"Hallucinations" (false responses) are an observed defect. Techniques to minimize and detect and counteract false responses are examined,

AI can detect a questioner's bias and return a response favorable to that bias. Examples and ways to avoid asking biased questions are presented and how to confirm the absence of bias in an AI response.

A real problem for resolution

A comparison is made with a known retrospective problem solution to a resolution made by AI.

The speed and comprehensiveness of the AI solution is dramatic compared to the retrospective solution. The comparison is essentially incomparable due to its scope and depth of analysis.

The methodologies described here are not presented as competing alternatives. They are complementary tools that can be applied individually or in combination depending upon the nature and complexity of the problem.

Chapter 1

Apollo Lunar Spacecraft Detonation Threat

Overview

The problem to be resolved was determination of the cause for small (100-pound-thrust) attitude control rocket detonation when using the hypergolic (reaction on contact) fuel/oxidizer propellant combination of Hydrazine (N_2H_4) and Nitrogen Tetroxide (N_2O_4) in a space-ambient environment. This fuel/oxidizer system was limited to the spacecraft Reaction Control System (RCS) attitude control system (roll, pitch and yaw).

This problem was presented under contract by NASA, Manned Spacecraft Center (MSC), Houston, Texas to the U. S. Bureau of Mines, Explosives Research Center, Pittsburgh, Pennsylvania for resolution. (Order No. T-39882(G)). The contract was for two years' duration, with the first six months for literature search followed by eighteen months practical investigation. The Bureau of Mines was chosen for this investigation because of its expertise in combustion phenomena. NASA suggested that the probability of detonation in an RCS engine was one in one million RCS engine firings.

This contract was initiated in 1965 and preceded many of the published works regarding problem resolution processes and techniques. A final report to NASA was issued by the U. S. Bureau of Mines, Explosives Research Center in 1967.

As steps taken to resolve this problem, the use the documentation techniques described in the Introduction will be utilized to capture the detail that ultimately resulted in resolution to the problem to the satisfaction of NASA. This retrospective review provides a vehicle to demonstrate the use of the disciplined structure for analyzing and resolving a problem.

D0: Ignition Delay Detonation in Apollo Lunar Spacecraft RCS Engines

D1: Select the Investigator(s)

H. Perlee (Research Chemist), T. Christos (Analytical Chemist), Y Miron (Chemical Engineer), H. James (Research Physicist)

D2: Describe the Problem

What: Preignition detonation in small 100-lb thrust attitude control rockets on the Apollo Lunar Spacecraft.

Where: Observed in tests conducted on earth in NASA Manned Spacecraft Center (MSC) vacuum chamber to simulate space-ambient conditions.

When: Tests conducted at MSC to evaluate performance of small 100-lb thrust attitude control rockets.

Who: NASA Manned Spacecraft Center.

How Big: Detonation rate estimated by MSC test results to be one in one million test firings.

Additional Information and Recorded Observations:

RCS thrusters were used only by and for their respective module needs. For example, the transition from Earth to Moon and return used the Service Module thrusters, the Lunar Module used RCS thrusters for descent to and return from the Lunar Surface, and the Command Module RCS thrusters were used only for re-entry to the Earth. Yet, this presented 44 opportunities for RCS thruster detonation.

Table 1: Total Number of RCS Thrusters Across Apollo Spacecraft:

Module	Number of RCS Thrusters	Purpose
Service Module	16 (4 quads × 4 jets)	Attitude + Translation Control
Lunar Module	16 (4 quads × 4 jets)	Attitude + Translation Control
Command Module	12 (2 systems × 6 jets)	Attitude Control Only
Total	44 RCS thrusters	Varies by phase/module use

Figure 1: Artist rendering of Apollo Spacecraft configuration in transit from Earth to Moon (courtesy NASA)

Figure 2: Lunar Module on the Moon: RCS Quad Engines are easily observed (courtesy NASA, apolloarchive.com, Index of Photographs, Apollo 11, Image ID AS11-40-5863-69 scan: Ed Hengeveld)

Investigative Direction from Literature Search Phase

The first six months of contract were devoted to a literature search, the full details of which are contained in a summary report (H. Perlee, et al. April 8 to December 31, 1965).

The purpose of the literature search was to delineate the physicochemical processes in hypergolic propellant engines that could be responsible for "hard start". Specifically, it was concerned with the processes that occur from the time of engine energization up to and including the "spike" phenomena. "Hard start" and "spike" were descriptive characterizations used by NASA to describe the events recorded during space-simulated environmental tests.

The events in the RCS rocket combustion chamber following fluid injection of the two propellants and prior to ignition are complicated by such factors as the distribution of droplet size and velocities in the spray, the effect of pressure, temperature, size and gas concentration (1) on the rate of droplet evaporation, (2) on the chemical and physical reactions, and (3) on the spatial and temporal dependence of fluid dynamics.

One cannot hope to factually delineate such a complex aggregate of processes but must contend with an overall understanding of the underlying mechanism to attack the problem for resolution.

The major focuses from a list of all related relevant processes were:

1. Physics of spray formation.
2. Hydrodynamics of fluid streams and jets in initially low-pressure environments.
3. Volatile liquid flow in initially low-pressure piping.
4. Heterogeneous pipe flow.
5. Hydrodynamic instability criteria of liquid jets.
6. Single particle physics.
7. Cooperative phenomena.
8. Drop kinematics.
9. Transport phenomena.
10. Physics of sprays.
11. Chemistry of combustion
12. Ignition.
13. Flame propagation.
14. Gas dynamics and transport.

From this search, a series of investigations were pursued to narrow down the resolution of the source of the observed deficiency.

What was known/observed?

MSC observed and measured ignition delays of 3 to 5 milliseconds when RCS engines were test fired at simulated space conditions, i.e., engine combustion chambers with pressures <0.05 psia.

Samples of residue from various internal engine surfaces (nozzle, combustion chamber, injector face, cooling shroud) and test chamber internal wall post firing were collected for analysis. The samples were typically less than one gram, each.

The samples were freeze dried to separate liquids from solid fractions. The liquid portions were always clear and colorless, and the solid portions were always a "straw yellow" color.

The liquid portions were analyzed by liquid chromatography. The solid portions were analyzed using infrared analysis.

The analysis demonstrated that the major constituents were water and hydrazine nitrate (HN).

D3: Develop Interim Containment Actions

NASA altered the fuel from Hydrazine to "Aerozine 50", a mixture of 50% Hydrazine and 50% Unsymmetrical Dimethyl Hydrazine (UDMH), and then to Monomethyl Hydrazine (MMH). Although NASA was satisfied that the change to MMH was to be the fuel used in the actual Apollo Lunar Mission, NASA wanted to investigate the detonation hazard represented by using Hydrazine as the fuel. This would aid in understanding space-ambient influence on future propellant options.

D4: Determine and Verify Root Causes

The six-month literature search was conducted to identify any studies of similar occurrences and to determine characteristics of Hydrazine and Nitrogen Tetroxide that would be important in formulating an experimental program to resolve the occurrence of "hard start, spiking" in the RCS engines.

Experiments to Evaluate Explanation for the Observed Results

Several hypotheses were considered and experimentally evaluated before the final root-cause mechanism was established.

Hypergolic-fueled rocket engines exhibit three successive stages in their operation: (1) the preignition or pressurization period during which the propellants are injected into the combustion chamber and are dispersed, vaporized and accelerated through the chamber; (2) the unilateral combustion stage during which a flame front starting at the ignition site initially traverses the combustible mixture; and (3) the steady state combustion process.

Only the first two stages are relevant to the hard start, spiking problem.

In space, the conditions are vastly different from those on Earth. Space is a near-perfect vacuum, with extremely low pressure and temperatures that can vary widely depending on the location and exposure to sunlight. In space, the lack of ambient pressure (near zero) and extreme temperatures (also near zero) mean that gases will expand to fill any available volume.

A 2D transparent engine was fabricated to simulate an RCS engine. The intent was to create a simple design to conduct experiments for visual and chemical analysis of the initial reactions. The propellant was injected into the chamber under vacuum conditions to measure the quantity of and the time period of the pulse cycle during which the HN was being formed. (Figure 2, H. Perlee et al., February 1968, pg. 233 and H. Perlee et al., April 1, 1965 to March 31, 1967, pg. 15a).

Four trials were conducted with each fuel (Hydrazine, Aerozine-50, UDMH and MMH) and oxidizer (Nitrogen Tetroxide (NTO)) combination. Injected propellant volumes were controlled, and propellant injection was approximately 5 milliseconds duration. With the benefit of transparency of the combustion chamber, a high-speed framing camera operating at approximately 5.000 frames per second was used to record the ignition event.

Figure 3: 2-D Plastic Engine

Following each test, approximately 0.1 milligram of residue was recovered from the combustion chamber walls and was subjected to infrared analysis.

The results showed the formation of the nitrate of each fuel in all combinations except with UDMH/NTO that formed Ammonium Nitrate (AN). AN was judged not to be as critical to this application as the nitrates of the other fuels. (H. Perlee, et al, April 1 to March 31, 1967, pg.16).

In a separate investigation, liquid films of HN/water and HN/N_2H_4 were demonstrated to support stable detonations in films as thin as 0.025 centimeters. (H. Perlee, et al, April 1 to March 31, 1967, pg.27).

Table 2: Detonation Velocities and Critical Film Thicknesses (cft) for Both Low Velocity and High Velocity Detonation for HN-water and HN-Hydrazine Solutions

Liquid Solution		Detonation Velocity			
		High Order		Low Order	
Composition	HN Concentration (weight percent)	Velocity (m/sec)	cft (cm)	Velocity (m/sec)	cft (cm)
HN	100	8,500	0.127	1,400	<0.025*
HN/H2O	85	7,600	0.305	2,400	<0.025
	75	Not Observed		2,100	0.330
	65	No Propogation			
HN/N2H4	80	8,600	0.076	1,800	
	60	8,200	0.076		
	40	7,800	0.254	2,200	
	20	No Propogation			

cft: Critical Film Thickness

0.025 cm apparatus resolution limit

Problem Resolution

Replace pure Hydrazine with Monomethyl Hydrazine (MMH).

Why It Worked

MMH has lower vapor pressure than hydrazine. It is more thermally stable, less volatile under vacuum, and reduces the likelihood of forming unstable intermediates that could lead to detonation. The MMH led to: (1) more uniform vaporization; (2) shorter and more reliable ignition delays; (3) reduced formation of transient detonation-sensitive intermediate.

By switching to a more stable propellant mixture, NASA effectively mitigated the risk of detonation, ensuring safer and more reliable operation of the attitude control rockets in space-ambient conditions. This underscores the importance of selecting appropriate propellant mixtures to balance performance with safety in space missions.

D5: Choose and Validate Permanent Corrective Actions

The discovery of residue of Hydrazine Nitrate in post-test analysis of the Hydrazine/Nitrogen Tetroxide in RCS testing was pivotal.

Moreover, detonation testing of HN in thin films confirmed the possibility for that sufficient material could accumulate to a point where detonation could occur.

The use of MMH and NTO throughout the remainder of the Apollo Lunar Spacecraft program demonstrated no incidents of malfunction of the RCS system.

D6: Implement Permanent Corrective Actions

The MMH/NTO propellant system was used successfully throughout the remainder of the Apollo Lunar program.

D7: Prevent Recurrence

The Hydrazine/Nitrogen Tetroxide propellant combination was abandoned for major NASA space-ambient RCS applications following these findings.

D8: Recognize Team and Individuals

The collective efforts and contributions of the team were recognized by the NASA and the members of the community of companies and organizations participating in the Apollo Space Program through the publication and acceptance of the findings resulting from the investigation into the cause for the preignition detonation in the RCS system.

Afterthoughts

The work cited here was done in the mid 1960s. Computers were just coming online (e.g., IBM 7090) and certainly no internet search engines existed at that time. A literature search of six months would not be remotely acceptable today. Six minutes might be acceptable today; six days likely would not.

Also, the breadth of the search engines today is far broader than anything available to this program.

Efficiency was not a major goal for completion of this investigation and problem resolution. NASA moved to fix the problem with the adoption of the MMH/NTO propellant system.

Moreover, analytical techniques that would be available today are faster and more comprehensive than those used during the era of this problem.

The 8D documentation format serves to keep everything together for control and review. Documents, such as laboratory reports and investigation summaries can be referenced in the 8D body and made as attachments to this form. This discipline keeps everything available for scrutiny as progress is made toward problem resolution.

The two factors leading to this decision were lower spiking frequency with less intensity due to a lower decomposition temperature and higher heat of combustion. This latter factor results in a larger chamber temperature increment per engine pulse. The lower decomposition temperature therefore leads to a lower potential accumulation of the monomethyl hydrazine nitrate (MN) below that necessary for extensive engine damage.

The Apollo spacecraft has forty-four (44) individual attitude control rockets (sixteen for the Service Module, sixteen for the Lunar Module and twelve for the Command Module). Given the experience in NASA's vacuum chamber tests and the one detonation experienced in the Bureau of Mines investigation, clearly Hydrazine as a space-ambient rocket fuel is unsatisfactorily risky. Only the methylated versions of Hydrazine are satisfactory for use.

Finally, the work done in this Apollo Mission investigation led to the adoption of MMH/NTO for the Space Shuttle Mission RCS system.

When a problem is inherently unsolvable, design it out.

Chapter 1 Bibliography

"Summary of Literature Survey of Hypergolic Ignition Spike Phenomena: Phase I – Final Report, No. 3982, April 8 to December 31, 1965" by Henry E. Perlee and Theodore Christos, United States Department of the Interior, Bureau of Mines, Pittsburgh, Pennsylvania for Manned Spacecraft Center, National Aeronautics and Space Administration, Houston Texas under Order No. T-39882(G).

"Exploratory Study of Hypergolic Ignition Spike Phenomena: Phase II – First Quarter Report, No. 3986, January 1 to March 31, 1966" by Theodore Christos, Yael Miron, Harry James and Henry E. Perlee, United States Department of the Interior, Bureau of Mines, Pittsburgh, Pennsylvania for Manned Spacecraft Center, National Aeronautics and Space Administration, Houston Texas under Order No. T-39882(G).

"Exploratory Study of Hypergolic Ignition Spike Phenomena: Phase II, Part II, July 1 to September 30, 1966" by Theodore Christos, Yael Miron, Harry James and Henry E. Perlee, United States Department of the Interior, Bureau of Mines, Pittsburgh, Pennsylvania for Manned Spacecraft Center, National Aeronautics and Space Administration, Houston Texas under Order No. T-39882(G).

"The Combustion Characteristics of Condensed Phase Aerozine-50/Nitrogen Tetroxide" by T Christos, Y. Miron, H. James, H. Perlee, Bureau of Mines, Department of the Interior, Pittsburgh, Pennsylvania, Interagency Chemical Rocket Propulsion Group, 3rd Combustion Conference, October 17-21, 1966, John F. Kennedy Space Center, NASA, Cocoa Beach, Florida.

"Hypergolic Ignition and Combustion Phenomena in the Propellant System Aerozine-50/N_2O_4, Quarterly Report, June 1 to August 31, 1967" by Henry E.

Perlee, Yael Miron and Harry James, United States Department of the Interior, Bureau of Mines, Pittsburgh, Pennsylvania for Manned Spacecraft Center, National Aeronautics and Space Administration, Houston Texas under Order No. T-39882(G).

"Hypergolic Ignition and Combustion Phenomena in the Propellant System Aerozine-50/N_2O_4, Final Report, No. 4019, April 1 to March 31, 1967" by Henry E. Perlee, Yael Miron, Harry James and Theodore Christos, United States Department of the Interior, Bureau of Mines, Pittsburgh, Pennsylvania for Manned Spacecraft Center, National Aeronautics and Space Administration, Houston Texas under Order No. T-39882(G).

"Combustion Characteristics of Condensed Phase Hydrazine-Type Fuels with Nitrogen Tetroxide" by T Christos, Y. Miron, H. James, H. Perlee, Journal of Spacecraft and Rockets, Volume 4, Number 9, September 1967, pp. 1224-1230.

"Preignition Phenomena in Small A-50/NTO Pulsed Rocket Engines" by H. E. Perlee, T Christos, Y. Miron, H. K. James, Journal of Spacecraft and Rockets, Volume 5, Number 2, February 1968, pp. 233-235.

Reply by Authors to C. W. Baulk night: Comments on "Preignition Phenomena in Small A-50/NTO Pulsed Rocket Engines" by H. E. Perlee, T Christos, Y. Miron, H. K. James, Journal of Spacecraft and Rockets, Volume 5, Number 2, February 1968, p. 1008.

"Physical and Combustion Characteristics of Hydrazine Nitrate" by Harry K. James, Yael Miron and Henry E. Perlee, Information Circular 8452, United States Department of the Interior, Bureau of Mines, March 1970.

"Apollo Experience Report – Command and Service Module Reaction Control Systems" by Ralph J. Taeuber and Dwayne P. Weury, Manned Spacecraft Center, Houston, Texas 77058, National Aeronautics and Space Administration, Washington, D.C, June 1973.

Chapter 2

Apollo 13 Emergency CO_2 Scrubber "Mailbox" Fix

Overview

Two days after Apollo 13 blasted off from Florida's Kennedy Space Center on April 11, 1970, an oxygen tank exploded in its Service Module, crippling its life support systems in the Command Module, forcing the crew (Jim Lovell, Jack Swigert, and Fred Haise) to move into the Lunar Module (LM) as a "lifeboat."

The Lunar Module's Environmental Control System was designed to support two astronauts for two days — but now it had to keep three astronauts alive for four or five days.

As the astronauts exhaled, carbon dioxide (CO_2) levels inside the LM began to rise dangerously. The LM's Lithium Hydroxide (LiOH) canisters, which absorbed CO_2, were not enough to last the extended time. There were more LiOH canisters available in the Command Module (CM), but they were physically incompatible; i.e., LM canisters were round, and CM canisters were square.

If they couldn't solve this, CO_2 poisoning would occur, leading to the astronauts' loss of consciousness and death.

NASA was forced to provide a method to overcome this deficiency by having a team on Earth determine how to use available components in the spacecraft to correct the problem.

D0: Apollo 13 Emergency CO_2 Scrubber "Mailbox" Fix

D1: Select the Investigator(s)

Robert E. "Ed" Smylie, NASA's Crew Systems/Life Support Engineering team leader.

James Correale, Deputy on Smylie's team

Joseph Kerwin (CAPCOM), Capsule Communicator for LM.

Deke Slayton, NASA's Director of Flight Crew Operations.

Mission Operations Support Teams (Johnson Space Center, Houston, Bldg. 30), ECS (Environmental Control System) engineers and staff support personnel, including Crew Systems Division, Life Support Systems Engineering Office, Flight controllers under the leadership of Flight Director Gene Kranz (White Team) and Glynn Lunney (Black Team), and NASA contractors (North American Rockwell, Grumman) provided technical support.

D2: Describe the Problem

What: Lunar Module Environmental Control System unable to maintain control of CO_2 balance threatening the lives of the three Apollo 13 astronauts.

Where: Apollo 13 Lunar Module.

When: Following the Service Module explosion and power down of the Command Module.

Who: Affected the lives of the Apollo 13 crew, Jim Lovell, Jack Swigert, and Fred Haise.

How Big: Death of the crew, if not corrected.

Additional Information and Recorded Observations:

The Apollo 13 Command Module (CM) was severely affected by the Service Module (SM) explosion on April 13, 1970. The blast critically damaged the CM's life support and power systems, forcing the three astronauts (Jim Lovell, Jack Swigert, and Fred Haise) to evacuate to the Lunar Module (LM), which then served as an improvised lifeboat.

D3: Develop Interim Containment Actions

The Service Module explosion forced the astronauts to move to the Lunar Module. The Command Module was powered down.

Summary: CM Damage and Crew Survival

1. Power: (fuel cells offline); Response: LM batteries used instead.
2. Oxygen: (tanks lost); Response: LM oxygen used for breathing.
3. Navigation: (no main computer); Response: LM systems used plus Earth-based trajectory planning.
4. Water: (no fuel cell production); Response: Conserved LM water & tolerated dehydration.
5. Heat: (risk of freezing); Response: Crew wore extra clothing, remained bundled together.
6. CO_2 Removal: (incompatibility); Response: Mission Control, primarily a group of engineers from the Life Support Systems team, worked under extreme time pressure to devise a solution using only materials available onboard Apollo 13.

NASA teams immediately compiled a "real-time inventory" from checklists, equipment manifests, and telemetry.

The following items onboard the spacecraft were identified for possible use. This inventory was pre-documented pre-launch and continuously referenced during flight operations

From the inventory list, they used the following items found aboard:
Plastic bags
Cardboard from flight manuals
Hose from a space suit
Duct tape (critical!)
Socks (as a secondary filter material)
The square CM Lithium Hydroxide (LiOH) canisters

The Apollo 13 crew had plenty of scrubbers for the Command Module but did not have backups for the lunar module. They were different shapes and sizes: the Lunar Module used cylindric scrubbers while the Command Module used cubic ones.

Led by "Ed" Smylie, NASA's engineers got to work to solve the problem:

1. How do we channel air flow from the LM's environmental fan through the square CM canister?
2. How do we seal all connections without welding or mechanical fittings?
3. How do we ensure astronauts can assemble this with gloved hands and no special tools?

This required the engineers in Houston to fashion a workaround that used the command module scrubbers in the lunar module. The NASA Team developed an improvised device nicknamed the "mailbox" because of its boxy, makeshift appearance.

How the NASA Team built the fix:

1. The Team taped a plastic bag around the square LiOH cartridge.
2. They then attached the hose from the LM's environmental system into the bag.
3. The airflow was forced through the canister, allowing it to absorb CO_2 despite the original mismatch in fittings.
4. Duct tape and cardboard provided structure to make it airtight.

The team assembled a physical prototype in the Lunar Module simulator at Building 7, Johnson Space Center. Materials were pulled from the astronaut training mockups (about 4 to 6 hours). Every step was tested and timed to ensure feasibility, and adjustments were made for fit, pressure seal, and flow rate (about 2 to 3 hours).

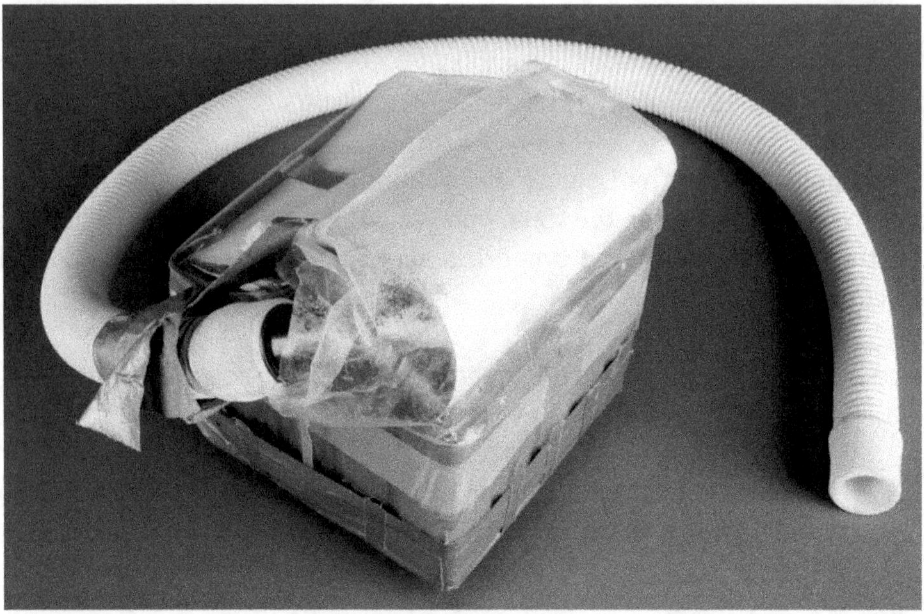

Figure 1: Emergency CO_2 Scrubber "Mailbox" The Apollo Lunar Surface Journal and Apollo Flight Journal; Apollo Program; Apollo 13; Apollo 13 Flight Journal – Day 4, Part 4: Building the CO_2 Adapter (courtesy NASA)

Final written instructions (requiring approximately one hour) were dictated over voice communications by CAPCOM Joseph Kerwin. Mission Control in Houston couldn't send pictures to the Apollo 13 crew, so Joe Kerwin's verbal clarity was essential to describe everything and hope the astronauts got the picture.

The astronauts constructed the device exactly per instruction in about an hour.

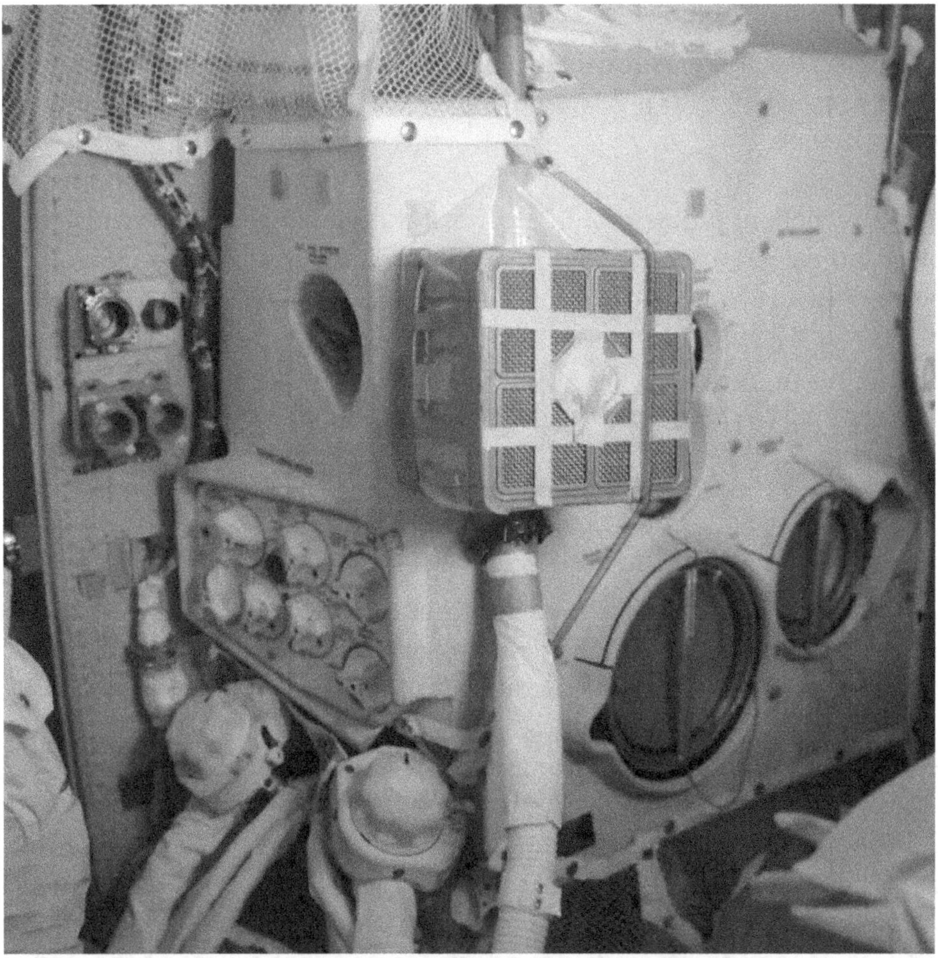

Figure 2: Emergency CO_2 Scrubber "Mailbox" Installed on Lunar Module (courtesy NASA, apolloarchive.com, Index of Photographs, Apollo 13, Image ID AS13-62-8929 scan: John Fongheiser)

CO_2 levels dropped rapidly after installation. The device functioned flawlessly for the remainder of the mission.

D4: Determine and Verify Root Causes

The failure of the Service Module induced the life-threatening CO_2 control problem that threatened the safe return of the Apollo 13 astronauts to Earth.

Root cause for the CO_2 control problem was the Service Module explosion that forced the three astronauts to be contained in the Lunar Module for four to five days, when the Lunar Module was designed for only two astronauts for two days' time.

The secondary problem of CO_2 control threatening the astronaut lives was solved on an interim basis until the other critical secondary problem of safe return of the astronauts to Earth after which only then could NASA review the total Apollo 13 problem.

What Happened: The Explosion and Immediate Effects

The cause of the Service Module explosion was a faulty thermostat switch which led to overheating during pre-launch tank operations.

When Tank 2 heater was turned on enroute to the Moon, it caused insulation failure and oxygen ignition. The resulting explosion blew off a panel of the SM and damaged. (See https://nasa.gov/history/afj/ap13fj/30postflight.html).

D5: Choose and Validate Permanent Corrective Actions

The permanent corrective action was to assure the Service Module functioned properly on all future Apollo Lunar Missions. This had to await the successful return of the Apollo astronauts to Earth.

These general target upgrades addressed the root causes of the Apollo 13 failure:

* Prevented high-voltage heater failures
* Improved oxygen system redundancy
* Enhanced wiring safety
* Boosted monitoring and life-support resilience

D6: Implement Permanent Corrective Actions

The corrective action to the Lunar Environmental System was only necessary for the time to allow return of the Apollo 13 crew to Earth alive.

The specific upgrades that were incorporated were:

1. Oxygen Tank Redesign

Upgrade of thermostatic switches to handle the full 65 V heater load (they had failed due to voltage that exceeded their rating). Conversion from aluminum to stainless-steel quantity probes, improving reliability and durability. Removal of internal stirring fans (their motors were unsealed and potentially hazardous), requiring flight rules changes.

2. Addition of a Third Oxygen Tank plus Isolation Valve

Installed in Bay 1, this extra tank provided redundancy and could be isolated in emergencies to feed only the Command Module via its own valve system.

3. Electrical and Safety Enhancements

All wiring in Bay 4 (the explosion site) was retrofitted with stainless-steel sheaths to prevent ignition in high-pressure oxygen environments. Fuel-cell supply valves were redesigned to better isolate sensitive wiring from oxygen flow. Enhanced monitoring added to spacecraft and Mission Control systems to deliver faster detection and clearer alerts for anomalies.

4. Improved Life-Support Backup Systems

A 5-gallon emergency water supply was added to the Command Module to address unexpected needs. An emergency silver-zinc battery, similar to the Lunar Module's, was included in the SM to support CM power needs. The LM was modified to simplify power transfer to the CM in emergencies.

5. Broader Modifications

Updates were made to the LM's descent-stage propellant tanks, including anti-slosh baffles to prevent false low-fuel indications.

These safety and reliability fixes were implemented and first applied starting with Apollo 14, ensuring lessons from Apollo 13 were incorporated into service module redesigns. No technical problems related to the cryogenic system, or the fuel cells were experienced.

D8: Recognize Team and Individuals

President Nixon presented the "Presidential Medal of Freedom" to the Apollo 13 Mission Operations Team, specifically naming Ed Smylie and James Correale for their leadership and ingenuity. It is one of the most famous and heroic engineering improvisations in spaceflight history!

Afterthoughts

It is important to recognize that CO_2 control was a secondary problem, but a life-threatening problem, nonetheless.

Another secondary life-threatening problem was how to get the astronauts back to Earth and safely recovered. These two problems took priority.

The real root problem was the failure of the Service Module that precipitated the secondary problems. Resolution to the root cause had to wait for the completion of the astronauts' safe recovery before diagnosis and corrective action to the Service Module and any identified for the Command and Lunar Modules.

It is still important to understand why this specific example matters: (1) It captures creativity under critical time constraint and solves the problem with only the materials on hand; (2) it demonstrates clear communication, i.e., Earth had to explain to the astronauts exactly how to build the device without diagrams — only through voice instructions; and (3) it demonstrates teamwork; I.e., cross-discipline engineers, from life support to mechanical systems, collaborated under pressure.

This problem resolution is also a good example for the need for timely written documentation. The process by which the available components were assembled had to be recreated by interviews with the team members after-the-fact to provide a written historical record of this critical process.

It remains one of the most famous real-world examples of applied engineering ingenuity under extreme time pressure, an iconic moment of engineering under duress.

A lesson from World War I and adopted in World War II was to design systems across the military branches that used common components, i.e., the JAN brand (Joint Army Navy). This lesson was primarily learned from the transportation vehicle experience of World War I when vehicles from different manufactures could not be repaired due to unique designs for each vehicle manufacturer. Repair parts had to be obtained from each vehicle manufacturer to affect repair/replacement. This lesson resulted in the JAN brand approach followed in World War II.

The Apollo Mission Spacecraft consisted of three modules, Service, Command and Lunar. Each module was designed by a separate outside contractor and NASA team due to the uniqueness of space application and complexity. It would have been beneficially good for the teams from each design to activity meet and discuss common system elements that could be identical across each module. This would have simplified the recovery of the CO_2 environmental control in the Lunar module with much greater efficiency. This might have avoided the “square pegs” (Command Module LiOH filters) and “round holes” (Lunar Module LiOH filters).

This example emphasizes the importance of Efficiency in problem resolution. Typically, problem resolution effectiveness is the foremost objective with sometimes little or no attention paid to efficiency (timeliness) in achieving resolution.

It was, in fact, a matter of life or death. There was no remote control to assure the return of Apollo 13 to Earth. It required the astronauts to carry out many series of actions to “fly” the spacecraft back to Earth. But they had to be alive to do that.

Efficiency is equal to Effectiveness for problems that threaten life or death consequences.

Chapter 2 Bibliography

The Apollo Lunar Surface Journal and Apollo Flight Journal (https://nasa.gov/history/afj/ap13fj/30postflight.html)

The Apollo Lunar Surface Journal and Apollo Flight Journal; Apollo Program; Apollo 13; Apollo 13 Flight Journal – Day 4, Part 4: Building the CO_2 Adapter (https://www.nasa.gov/history/afj/ap13fj/15day4-mailbox.html)

Apollo 13 by Jim Lovell and Jeffrey Kluger, Mariner Books, 2006, ISBN 978-0-618-61958-0

Failure is Not an Option: Mission Control from Mercury to Apollo 13 and Beyond by Gene Kranz, Simon and Shuster Paperbacks, 2000, ISBN 978-1-4391-4881-5

Chapter 3

Profitability in a Manufacturing Operation

Overview

The problem presented in this chapter is the result of perceptive failure to achieve expected, acceptable profitability in an ongoing manufacturing operation.

There was a significant amount of objective sales data history from which to determine a cause for insufficient profitability and several alternatives to correct for the determined cause. This problem is a decade old retrospective analysis but could be easily adaptable to a current situation.

The challenge occurred after the acquisition of the company and management replacement.

How to approach a large set of data to determine what drives the root source of the problem is demonstrated.

D0: Profitability in a Manufacturing Operation

D1: Select the Investigator(s)
Harry K. James, General Manager, Principal Investigator/Analyst

D2: Describe the Problem
What: In three business years, the company was barely profitable. The product is high reliability (HiRel) discrete transistor semiconductor devices supplying the military, aerospace and space communities, a small, specialized market segment.

Discrete transistors were the first use of planar semiconductor technology that became standard processing technology for integrated circuits that are used by the millions in electronic devices today.

This specific market segment is subjected to U. S. Government Agency oversight to assure conformance to documented certification of products offered to this segment customer base. Regular government agency review and audits are normal processes. A request for bid for any product appearing on the Qualified Parts List (QPL) published by the Agency must receive a valid response. A "no-bid" will result in Agency removal of the requested part from the QPL. If a product was desired by a customer that required performance differing from the QPL requirements, a customer could request an SCD (a Source (Customer) Controlled Drawing) device, unique to the customer's requirements.

Product is manufactured in batch lots according to the number of parts on order by customer. High reliability discipline requires process monitoring throughout the manufacturing process to assure that parts manufactured at the beginning of the process do not deviate from final acceptance during the batch manufacturing process. During the process, devices are subjected to specific destructive tests to assure conformance and are retained and not shipped with the lot.

Perfection does not exist in the semiconductor industry regardless of market segment served. The primary focus of every semiconductor manufacturing operation is yield: how many parts were started and how many parts were successfully finished. Yield is the prime directive for cost performance. There are many other cost drivers, but every semiconductor manufacturer measures this one.

Semiconductor manufacturing operational groups are generally separated into three operating units: wafer fabrication, assembly and test.

The manufacture of semiconductor devices is both an art and a science. The science is in the device physics for design, but the art is in the equipment used to achieve the device physics performance. Product in this discrete device segment has an over fifty years' history of successful device performance.

For these discrete devices, Wafer Fabrication requires a starting wafer, a mask set, high temperature furnaces, photolithographic processes, and metal plating processes to achieve functional performance.

Groups of ten wafers per design are started and each wafer for this type of device can yield 18,000 good dies per four-inch diameter wafer. While wafer fabrication is costly, there is little material cost differences recorded lot-to-lot. That is, nothing unlikely tends to occur.

Semiconductor Assembly operations are where most aberrations in process can occur. The personnel who perform these operational functions are well trained (to assure yield performance) and historically do not hesitate to notify supervisory personnel when "something is not right". For this manufacturing plant, there are multiple assembly process steps that require individual operator attention. Some of these processes are manual (operator controlled) and some are mechanized (machine controlled with operator oversight). None are automated.

Test operations can require manual testing under operator control for unique tests or can utilize a mechanized test systems if justified by volume.

For all three manufacturing groups, process records must be retained for at least five years.

Where: A single facility that included all manufacturing and sales and general administrative support.

When: Over a period of three successive years.

Who: A manufacturing and support staff of approximately eighty (80) employees.

How Big: Product Sales for the three years totaled approximately $46 million. Profit for the three years was less than $1.5 million.

Additional Information and Recorded Observations:

It is necessary to understand an Income Statement to look for inconsistencies that may be the source of poor profit performance. The classical manufacturing operation Income Statement is shown below:

Income Statement
For the Year Ended [Date]

Sales Revenue			
Net Sales			$ [Amount]
Cost of Goods Sold			
Beginning Finished Goods Inventory		$ [Amount]	
Cost of Goods Manufactured (refer to separate schedule)		$ [Amount]	
Cost of Goods Available for Sale		$ [Amount]	
Ending Finished Goods Inventory		$ [Amount]	
Cost of Goods Sold			$ [Amount]
Gross Profit			$ [Amount]
Gross Profit Margin			% [Percent of Sales]
Operating Expenses			
Selling Expenses			
Sales Salaries	$ [Amount]		
Advertising Expense	$ [Amount]		
Delivery Expense	$ [Amount]		
Total Selling Expenses		$ [Amount]	
General and Administrative Expenses			
Office Salaries	$ [Amount]		
Rent Expense (Allocated)	$ [Amount]		
Utilities Expense (Allocated)	$ [Amount]		
Total General and Administrative Expenses		$ [Amount]	
Total Operating Expenses			$ [Amount]
Operating Income			$ [Amount]
Other Income and Expenses			
Interest Income	$ [Amount]		
Interest Expense	$ [Amount]		
Gain/Loss on Sale of Assets	$ [Amount]		
Net Other Income/Expenses			$ [Amount]
Income Before Tax			$ [Amount]
Income Tax Expense			$ [Amount]
Net Income			$ [Amount]
Net Income Profit Margin			% [Percent of Sales]

Note: This is a simplified example. Real-world income statements often contain more detailed breakdowns and classifications, especially in larger, more complex manufacturing operations. One can prepare a traditional income statement by choosing a reporting period, adding up total revenue, adding up the Cost of Goods Sold (COGS), calculating gross profit, calculating operating expenses, calculating income, calculating interest and taxes, and discovering net income.

Note: A "material" cost item in accounting terminology means that a value is of sufficient importance that a decision maker would consider it when judging the performance of a business entity. Some values are immaterial and therefore do not influence a decision on performance. Typically, a deviation in a financial performance parameter of five percent or less is not considered material.

There are "Rules-of-Thumb" in a manufacturing operation that represent acceptable levels or unacceptable levels of financial expectation performance. In this problem, there are two which stand out from others: Gross Profit Margin and Net Income.

In a manufacturing operation, Gross Profit Margin should exceed 65% of Net Sales and Net Income and should be between 8% and 12% of Net Sales. In each case, if the value exceeded these numbers, that would represent better than expected performance.

In this example, The Net Sales and the Net Profit are given. The Gross Margin is not yet identified. From the initial measures presented, Net Sales for Product is $46 million and for Net Income the number is $1.5 million. This profit represents 3.2% of Sales. This value is obviously well below the minimum expected of a manufacturing operation. This by itself is sufficient grounds to ask the question prompted in the initial problem statement.

Manufacturing Variances

There are manufacturing variances for Material, Labor and Overhead. These variances recognize differences for these three categories in planned cost expectations from actual costs incurred to perform the operation. They can be favorable (less than expected cost) or unfavorable (more than expected cost).

Material Variances

These measure the difference between the **standard cost of materials** (what materials *should* have cost) and the **actual cost** (what they *did* cost).

1. **Material Price Variance (MPV)** shows whether materials were purchased at a higher or lower price than expected: (Actual Price – Standard Price) × Actual Quantity.
2. **Material Quantity (or Usage) Variance (MQV)** indicates whether the production process used more or less material than the standard allows: (Actual Quantity – Standard Quantity) × Standard Price.

Labor Variances

These analyze the difference between the **standard labor cost** (based on expected rates and hours) and the **actual labor cost**.

1. **Labor Rate Variance (LRV)** measures if workers were paid more or less per hour than planned: (Actual Rate – Standard Rate) × Actual Hours.
2. **Labor Efficiency Variance (LEV)** evaluates whether labor took more or fewer hours than expected to produce the actual output: (Actual Hours – Standard Hours) × Standard Rate.

Overhead Variances

These compare the **actual overhead costs** with the **standard (or applied) overhead** based on production activity.

1. **Variable Overhead Spending Variance** reflects whether variable overhead costs were higher or lower than expected per hour: Actual Variable Overhead – (Actual Hours × Standard Variable Overhead Rate).
2. **Variable Overhead Efficiency Variance** measures the efficiency of using the activity base (often labor hours or machine hours): (Actual Hours – Standard Hours) × Standard Variable Overhead Rate.

3. **Fixed Overhead Spending (or Budget) Variance** shows if fixed overhead costs were over- or under-spent compared to the budget: Actual Fixed Overhead – Budgeted Fixed Overhead.
4. **Fixed Overhead Volume Variance** indicates whether production volume was above or below expected levels—spreading fixed costs over more or fewer units: Budgeted Fixed Overhead – Standard Fixed Overhead Applied to Actual Output.

Material and Labor Variances are typically captured because the components are more objectively recorded. Materials are purchasing and inventory measured and labor hours are recorded for payroll.

Overhead Variances can receive less attention and review because the underlying variable and fixed overhead rates require detailed development and allocation analysis. This requires a cost accounting expertise to prepare this analysis. A good shop floor reporting system and financial accounting system is important in aiding this analysis, but it also requires the cost accountant to be very familiar with the product flow and supporting functions.

The Problem Statement:

If Net Income were 10% of Net Sales, a profit of $4.6 million would be realized. What is contributing to reduced profit?

This prompts an Ishikawa "Fish Bone" Analysis aid for focus.

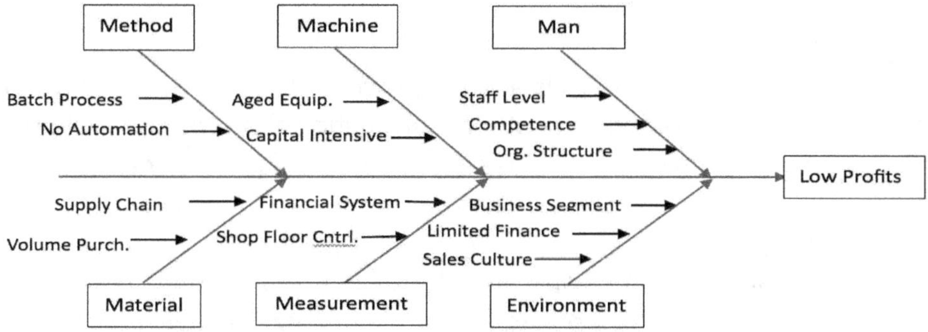

D3: Develop Interim Containment Actions

Until the analysis of profitability could be completed, no actions to mitigate the concern for profitability were proposed. It was felt that, without analytical review, any actions taken could exacerbate the already lean performance.

D4: Determine and Verify Root Causes

From the Ishikawa "Fish Bone" diagram and the possible manufacturing variances, a review is conducted to assess the ranking importance to the items listed to profitability. Competence to produce the product was more than favorable as many outside audits were complimentary to the work force skills evaluations.

Man:

The staffing level is a cost contributor but was judged to be adequate and not underutilized. In fact, there was material labor overtime payment. The organizational structure was very representative of a classical manufacturing operation. Labor rate cost is stable over this time period. Labor hour efficiency is consistent with lot-to-lot production volume.

Machine:

This manufacturing process is very capital intensive; each piece of equipment is specialized to perform its function. The process is recognized as an old process, and the equipment is also aged. Nevertheless, the equipment is well maintained and there is no evidence that equipment downtime was in any way material to the manufacturing performance.

Method:

The manufacturing process is a batch process. Parts move as a group from one manufacturing station to another. Automating this process would require more capital than could be raised based on the financial performance exhibited.

Material:

The materials used in this operation have been and continue to be available from an established industry-wide supply chain. The Purchasing function was well versed in volume purchasing supply agreements. Materials purchasing cost is stable. Yield performance shows no evidence of materials usage variance.

Measurement:

There was no evidence of extensive performance monitoring, either financial or manufacturing. There was no shop floor control system in use by this operation. The fact that profitability was called in to question was the result of the absence of this monitoring.

Environment:

As noted earlier, this business segment is small serving the military, aerospace and space government contractors. Its products have special utilization in the systems produced by these contractors. Entry by new suppliers is prohibitively capital intensive. Profit generation is judged to be prohibitive to major process enhancement. Sales culture is very top-line focused.

Given the Ishikawa and manufacturing variances analysis, it appears that sales history is the place to start since product demand and contribution to sales is the first step to understanding how the operation is meeting supply to match the demand and generate profit. The first evident need-to-know is product mix: what was sold, how many, what was the contribution to revenue?

Given the little analytical evidence available, a basic question is "what is being sold" and at "what volumes"?

What other relevant information/data is available for analysis:

1. Revenue by sales order line item for each part number for each of the three years.
2. Internal device type for each part number shipped was recorded.
3. External package type for each part number shipped was recorded.

The record for each revenue year, an Excel Spreadsheet, included the following titled relevant columns:

1. Revenue Type: (1) Product (Qualified Parts List (QPL) devices), (2) Service (outside test, process data records), (3) New Items (customer Source Controlled Drawings (SCDs))
2. Part Number
3. Part Description
4. Package Type
5. Device Type
6. Customer
7. GL (General Ledger) Quarter
8. GL Year
9. QTY (Quantity)
10. Unit Price
11. Revenue (Total Order Value)

The three years of listed sales transactions accumulated 10,110 entry lines. These records provide the details necessary to assess product contribution and mix for analysis. The year-to-year difference in order rate was immaterial.

The following steps are to be taken to subject this large data base of information for analysis:

1. Combine the three years' sales data into one spreadsheet.
2. Determine which sorting measures to subject the combined spreadsheet for more clarifying details.
    a. Sort by Revenue Type: New Item/Service versus Product
        i. New item: 194 Line items @ $1,542,249 ($7,949.73 per line item)
        ii. Service Item: 1861 Line Items @ $4,935,040 ($2,651.82 per line item)
        iii. Product Item: 8055 Line Items @ $46,250,852 ($5,741.88 per line item)
    b. Total Three-Year Revenue Line Items: 10,110
3. "New" Line Items are marked up at two times the Manufacturing Overhead Cost to load the requirements into the Manufacturing System and do not have any material detrimental effect on profitability

4. "Service" Line Items are also marked up two time the cost for the outside test service requested by the customer as part the product order and do not have any material detrimental effect on profitability.

As noted above, there are over 8,000 Product Line Items for analysis. This is more than can be conveniently presented here. Before these analytical processes are applied to the real Excel spreadsheet, a simulated example for how this analytical process is demonstrated. The process steps delineated for this example are the same as applied to the real Excel spreadsheet and would apply to any analysis of this type.

This process is demonstrated in the Appendix labeled "Simulation Example" at the end of this chapter.

There are three identified product types that generate revenue: "Product", "Service" and "New". A quick inspection of the three-years' Excel spreadsheet indicates a lot more sales action for "Product" than for either "Service" or "New". The first thing to arrange is consolidation of these three classes into three separate groups.

Then, determine if all groups have material impact to the total revenue for choice on which to focus.

Consideration of "New" and "Service" revenue is removed from further consideration. "New" revenue accounts for $1,542,249 and "Service" revenue accounts for $4,935,040, 2.9% and 9.6%, respectively of the total Revenue of $52,728,141. Since both Product Types do not require manufacturing capacity and are assured by their pricing to be very profitable, no further consideration is needed.

The three-year data base is then sorted by specific product yielding 257 Product (Part Numbers) of specific product designation accounting for $46,250,852.

The 257-line items are then sorted from highest revenue per part number to lowest revenue per part number.

The revenue is accumulated by line item, first to account for 80% of total revenue, then for 90% of total revenue, then for 95% of revenue, the last group of line items accounting for the last 5% of total revenue.

A group chosen for more detailed review can then be further segregated (1) by part number and (2) subtotaled for part number contribution to revenue and then (3) arranged in hierarchical order for its revenue contribution. Identify the inconsistencies in the resulting data.

Table 1: Hierarchical Revenue Order

Revenue Level	80% Revenue	>80% to 90% Revenue	>90% to 95% Revenue	>95% to 100% Revenue	Totals
Revenue	$37,031,899	$4,581,698	$2,330,145	$2,327,049	$46,250,852
Part Numbers	32	27	33	165	257
% Part Numbers	12.5%	10.5%	12.8%	64.2%	100.0%
Total Units	3,679,861	907,056	233,214	273,918	5,093,298
ASP*	$10.06	$5.05	$9.99	$8.50	$9.08
Averaga Qty	115,000	33,600	7,100	1,700	
* ASP: Average Sales Price					

A chart derived from the table of Revenue by level and number of Part Numbers is shown in Figure 1.

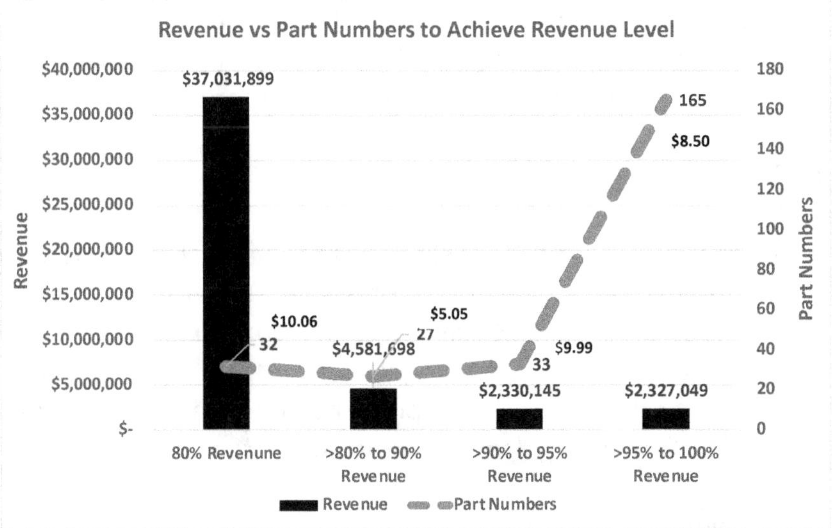

Figure 1: Revenue by Level and Number of part Numbers

It is clear from the table that if there were any economies-of-scale manufacturing, they were catastrophically diluted by the volume of small orders. The graphical representation is even more emphatic.

And the fact that a purchaser could get essentially the same price per part at 1,000 pieces as at 10,000 pieces is further catastrophic to production efficiency and profitability.

A major revision is required for order entry acceptance and volume dependent pricing.

D5: Choose and Validate Permanent Corrective Actions

Corrective action for a problem of this type takes time to implement and to see results. It is not demonstrable overnight. In the specific market segment presented here where lead times for order entry to customer delivery can be as long as twenty-six weeks with payment some thirty days more, one has to wait a significant delayed timeline to see the results come to fruition.

The existing Sales philosophy that all requests for purchase shall be automatically accepted is destructive. Small quantity orders must have a revised process for acceptance. The first thing to correct is pricing.

Learning Curve Pricing

A "learning curve" is a graphical representation that shows how performance improves with experience, practice, or time spent on a task.

1. The "horizontal axis (X-axis)" usually represents "time", "cumulative production units", or "repetitions".
2. The "vertical axis (Y-axis)" represents "performance metrics", such as "speed", "accuracy", "cost per unit", or "error rate".

At the beginning, improvements tend to be "steep and rapid" as people or systems pick up new skills or refine processes; over time, the curve "flattens out" as gains become harder to achieve.

When applied to pricing, learning curve pricing starts out higher at low volume purchasing and decreases by a fixed percentage as volume doubles.

Pricing learning curves typically exhibit declining pricing as order volume increases.

If, for example, pricing was being considered for tractor sales, the order volume for this type of high cost, low volume product would be shallow. If one tractor is sold for $10,000 each, two tractors sold might sell for $9,500 each. That is a 95% learning curve result.

Higher volume items tend to have more aggressive learning curves.

In the commercial semiconductor segment, a learning curve of 80% in not untypical. As an example, a semiconductor device purchase at a volume of 5,000 units might sell for a price of $10.00 per unit. An order for double that volume, or 10,000 units, would sell for a price of $8.00.

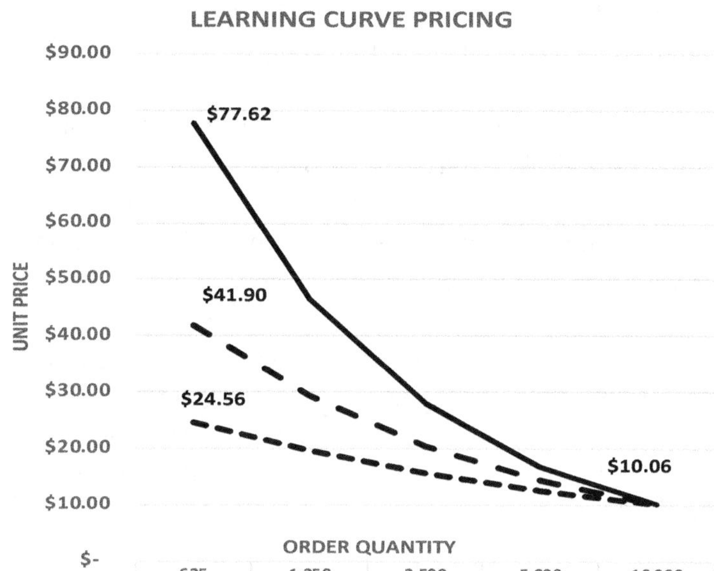

	625	1,250	2,500	5,000	10,000
80%	$24.56	$19.65	$15.72	$12.58	$10.06
70%	$41.90	$29.33	$20.53	$14.37	$10.06
60%	$77.62	$46.57	$27.94	$16.77	$10.06

Figure 2: Learning Curve Pricing

This product segment is not considered a commercial product. It is a high reliability product requiring stringent controls to assure long term field use in military, aerospace and space applications.

As such, there is significant cost differential from commercial grade semiconductors, mainly in overhead cost for process monitoring activities.

These costs would be attributed proportionally to the order volume. The proportional cost to each manufactured unit would be higher for low volume order and should be lower for high volume pricing.

D6: Implement Permanent Corrective Actions
Adjust pricing to reflect the volume dependence of order size.

A 70% learning curve for pricing is the best choice subject to future analysis that may require adjustment. The prices identified on the 70% learning curve should be treated as guides, since the Average Selling Prices (ASPs) at the quantity break points are averages. Each device type has a potential material difference in the Bill-of-Materials cost or additional equipment requirements for assembly and/or test. These differences require that careful consideration be given. It is not uncommon for there to be negotiation between customer and supplier to arrive at an agreed upon unit price.

The obvious goal is not to lose money on an order. It is very likely that under the former pricing strategy, significant unfavorable overhead variances were absorbed for Variable Overhead Spending Variance (overtime premium) and Fixed Overhead Volume Variance (inefficiency due to small lot sizes) were experienced.

Senior Management reviewed with a revised appreciation for volume pricing to assure that any small orders are worthy of acceptance for profitability. Initially, small orders of 2,500 units or less were subjected to this review.

Senior Management will determine when small order devices shall be voluntarily removed from the Government Qualified Parts List.

A Senior Management quarterly review was instituted to track modified performance. Any adjustments can be made under this due diligence review.

At a point when financial results show an annualized profit performance of eight percent (8%) or more of Net Sales, procurement of a comprehensive shop floor software and hardware system will be initiated.

A cost accounting specialist was to be contracted to assist the establishment of a cost accounting system necessary to capture real time cost for the benefit of informed review of financial performance.

D7: Prevent Recurrence

Actions taken above are designed to prevent recurrence. The Quarterly review by Senior Management was instituted to maintain focus and adjust as evidence determines the need.

Policy changes to order entry: review and adjust pricing to assure revenue sufficient to justify taking the order.

D8: Recognize Team and Individuals

No recognition is/was necessary. It is just a case of doing what should be expected of business leadership to assure business continuity and growth.

Afterthoughts

To describe previous owners and its management as derelict is far too kind. This analysis could have been done after the first year of the three presented here and would have identified the same weakness. Corrective action could easily have been taken to alter the profitability for the next two years before it became necessary to divest the operation.

If the marketplace dictated the price for small quantities, it does not follow that the business must follow the marketplace. Particularly, if doing so, significantly reduces profit. In the case presented, taking these small orders completely undercut economies-of-scale and only contributed five (5) percent of the total income while representing almost two thirds of the specific part number sales.

And while it was politically incorrect to no-bid the low volume product, nothing prevented the bid from being large enough to dissuade the customer from placing the order and to place it with the competition and causing the competition to sacrifice profit when taking the order at that market price.

As further validation of the corrective action, this business entity was acquired by a public company.

If you don't know your costs, you are – by definition – out of control.

Chapter 3 Appendix

Simulation Example

This simulated database is a much smaller database that demonstrates the steps necessary to segregate and isolate summaries of the data necessary to aid in identifying elements that can clarify contributors to problem understanding, analysis and then point to steps for resolution of the stated problem.

The titles for columns in the table below are the same as in the real database. The row entries are not from the real database but are close simulations to that data.

Simulated Database

Revenue Type	Part Number	Part Description	Package Type	Die Geometry	Customer Group	Commission Amount	GL Quarter	GL Year	QTY	Unit Price	Revenue
N	X0011	X20011	D2	0011	C001	$0.00	1Q'10	2010	175	$145.00	$25,375.00
P	X2907	X20600	T180	0600	A001	$0.00	1Q'10	2010	25000	$1.30	$32,500.00
P	X2907	X20600	T720	0006	A001	$0.00	1Q'10	2010	1000	$22.50	$22,500.00
P	X3507	X21506	T390	1506	A001	$0.00	1Q'10	2010	500	$6.00	$3,000.00
P	X3735	X20806	T390	0806	A001	$0.00	1Q'10	2010	1000	$4.80	$4,800.00
P	X3700	X24500	CS	4500	A001	$0.00	1Q'10	2010	1000	$7.00	$7,000.00
P	X2857	X20011	TY720	0011	A001	$0.00	1Q'10	2010	1000	$18.50	$18,500.00
P	X0918	X20003	T720	0003	A001	$0.00	1Q'10	2010	100	$13.50	$1,350.00
P	X2222	X20400	T180	0400	A001	$0.00	1Q'10	2010	2000	$4.75	$9,500.00
P	X3506	X21506	T390	1506	A001	$0.00	1Q'10	2010	500	$6.00	$3,000.00
P	X3700	X24500	T180	4500	A001	$0.00	1Q'10	2010	2000	$2.80	$5,600.00
P	X4261	X20014	T720	0014	A001	$0.00	1Q'10	2010	1000	$17.25	$17,250.00
P	X5109	X21009	T390	1009	A001	$0.00	1Q'10	2010	500	$18.50	$9,250.00
P	X2222	X20400	T180	0400	A001	$0.00	1Q'10	2010	10000	$1.30	$13,000.00
P	X2907	X20600	CS	0600	S001	$0.00	1Q'10	2010	50	$9.20	$460.00
P	X3705	X24500	CS	4500	S001	$0.00	1Q'10	2010	50	$9.42	$471.00
P	X9702	X29702	T390	9702	G001	$5,123.39	1Q'10	2010	370	$276.94	$102,467.80
S	LEAD FINISH	Charge	Charge	Charge	G001	$5,123.39	1Q'10	2010	370	$0.00	$0.00
P	X2222	X20400	T180	0400	C002	$172.50	1Q'10	2010	100	$10.25	$1,025.00
S	SPECIAL TEST	Charge	Charge	Charge	C002	$172.50	1Q'10	2010	1	$1,500.00	$1,500.00
S	CD DATA DISK	Charge	Charge	Charge	C002	$172.50	1Q'10	2010	1	$925.00	$925.00
P	X2222	X20400	T180	0400	R001	$0.00	1Q'10	2010	4000	$3.75	$15,000.00
S	CD DATA DISK	Charge	Charge	Charge	R001	$0.00	1Q'10	2010	1	$1,000.00	$1,000.00
S	SPECIAL TEST	Charge	Charge	Charge	R001	$0.00	1Q'10	2010	1	$500.00	$500.00
P	X29700	X209700	T390	9700	A001	$0.00	1Q'10	2010	200	$5.89	$1,178.00
N	X20006	X20006	D2	0006	M001	$0.00	1Q'10	2010	200	$16.44	$3,288.00
P	X8085	X28085	LC3	8085	H001	$0.00	1Q'10	2010	60	$9.83	$589.80
	Note: This sample does not incorporate the actual database										

The first step in the process to analyze the data is to group the revenue types. As in the actual database, there are three revenue types: N, P and S.

N represents simulated New products, P represents existing Products and S represents Special requirements to fulfill the customer order. The meaning for these three designations is the same as described in D4 of the 8D document above.

The Excel screenshot below shows the method for sorting the data by Revenue Type.

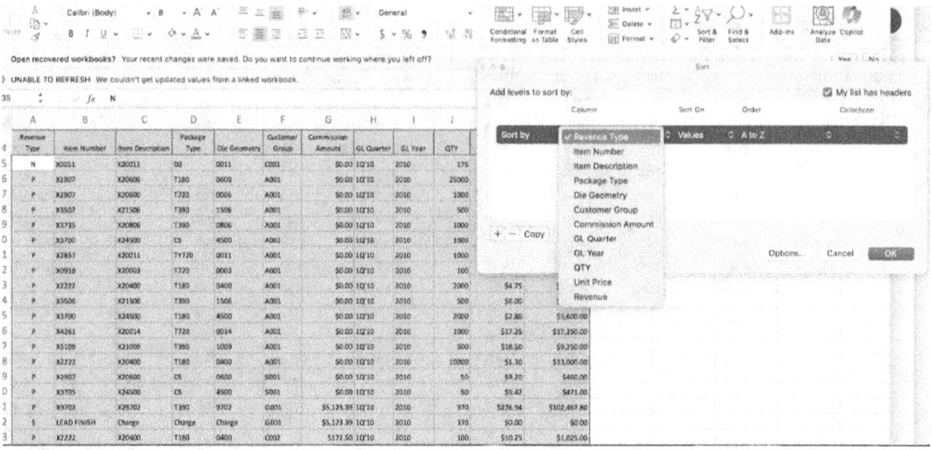

Excel demonstration for Sorting by Revenue Type

Spreadsheet sorted by Revenue Type

Revenue Type	Part Number	Part Description	Package Type	Die Geometry	Customer Group	Commission Amount	GL Quarter	GL Year	QTY	Unit Price	Revenue
N	X0011	X20011	D2	0011	C001	$0.00	1Q'10	2010	175	$145.00	$25,375.00
N	X20006	X20006	D2	0006	M001	$0.00	1Q'10	2010	200	$16.44	$3,288.00
P	X2907	X20600	T180	0600	A001	$0.00	1Q'10	2010	25000	$1.30	$32,500.00
P	X2907	X20600	T720	0006	A001	$0.00	1Q'10	2010	1000	$22.50	$22,500.00
P	X3507	X21506	T390	1506	A001	$0.00	1Q'10	2010	500	$6.00	$3,000.00
P	X3735	X20806	T390	0806	A001	$0.00	1Q'10	2010	1000	$4.80	$4,800.00
P	X3700	X24500	CS	4500	A001	$0.00	1Q'10	2010	1000	$7.00	$7,000.00
P	X2857	X20011	TY720	0011	A001	$0.00	1Q'10	2010	1000	$18.50	$18,500.00
P	X0918	X20003	T720	0003	A001	$0.00	1Q'10	2010	100	$13.50	$1,350.00
P	X2222	X20400	T180	0400	A001	$0.00	1Q'10	2010	2000	$4.75	$9,500.00
P	X3506	X21506	T390	1506	A001	$0.00	1Q'10	2010	500	$6.00	$3,000.00
P	X3700	X24500	T180	4500	A001	$0.00	1Q'10	2010	2000	$2.80	$5,600.00
P	X4261	X20014	T720	0014	A001	$0.00	1Q'10	2010	1000	$17.25	$17,250.00
P	X5109	X21009	T390	1009	A001	$0.00	1Q'10	2010	500	$18.50	$9,250.00
P	X2222	X20400	T180	0400	A001	$0.00	1Q'10	2010	10000	$1.30	$13,000.00
P	X2907	X20600	CS	0600	S001	$0.00	1Q'10	2010	50	$9.20	$460.00
P	X3705	X24500	CS	4500	S001	$0.00	1Q'10	2010	50	$9.42	$471.00
P	X9702	X29702	T390	9702	G001	$5,123.39	1Q'10	2010	370	$276.94	$102,467.80
P	X2222	X20400	T180	0400	C002	$172.50	1Q'10	2010	100	$10.25	$1,025.00
P	X2222	X20400	T180	0400	R001	$0.00	1Q'10	2010	4000	$3.75	$15,000.00
P	X29700	X209700	T390	9700	A001	$0.00	1Q'10	2010	200	$5.89	$1,178.00
P	X8085	X28085	LC3	8085	H001	$0.00	1Q'10	2010	60	$9.83	$589.80
S	LEAD FINISH	Charge	Charge	Charge	G001	$5,123.39	1Q'10	2010	370	$0.00	$0.00
S	SPECIAL TEST	Charge	Charge	Charge	C002	$172.50	1Q'10	2010	1	$1,500.00	$1,500.00
S	CD DATA DISK	Charge	Charge	Charge	C002	$172.50	1Q'10	2010	1	$925.00	$925.00
S	CD DATA DISK	Charge	Charge	Charge	R001	$0.00	1Q'10	2010	1	$1,000.00	$1,000.00
S	SPECIAL TEST	Charge	Charge	Charge	R001	$0.00	1Q'10	2010	1	$500.00	$500.00

Note: This sample does not incorporate the actual database

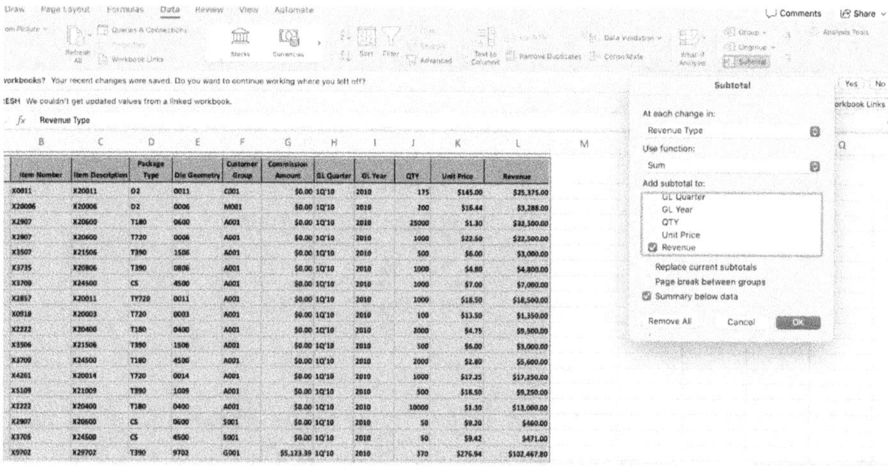

Excel Demonstration for Subtotaling Revenue Types

Spreadsheet Subtotaled for Revenue Type

Revenue Type	Part Number	Part Description	Package Type	Die Geometry	Customer Group	Commission Amount	GL Quarter	GL Year	QTY	Unit Price	Revenue
N	X0011	X20011	D2	0011	C001	$0.00	1Q'10	2010	175	$145.00	$25,375.00
N	X20006	X20006	D2	0006	M001	$0.00	1Q'10	2010	200	$16.44	$3,288.00
N Total											$28,663.00
P	X2907	X20600	T180	0600	A001	$0.00	1Q'10	2010	25000	$1.30	$32,500.00
P	X2907	X20600	T720	0006	A001	$0.00	1Q'10	2010	1000	$22.50	$22,500.00
P	X3507	X21506	T390	1506	A001	$0.00	1Q'10	2010	500	$6.00	$3,000.00
P	X3735	X20806	T390	0806	A001	$0.00	1Q'10	2010	1000	$4.80	$4,800.00
P	X3700	X24500	CS	4500	A001	$0.00	1Q'10	2010	1000	$7.00	$7,000.00
P	X2857	X20011	TY720	0011	A001	$0.00	1Q'10	2010	1000	$18.50	$18,500.00
P	X0918	X20003	T720	0003	A001	$0.00	1Q'10	2010	100	$13.50	$1,350.00
P	X2222	X20400	T180	0400	A001	$0.00	1Q'10	2010	2000	$4.75	$9,500.00
P	X3506	X21506	T390	1506	A001	$0.00	1Q'10	2010	500	$6.00	$3,000.00
P	X3700	X24500	T180	4500	A001	$0.00	1Q'10	2010	2000	$2.80	$5,600.00
P	X4261	X20014	T720	0014	A001	$0.00	1Q'10	2010	1000	$17.25	$17,250.00
P	X5109	X21009	T390	1009	A001	$0.00	1Q'10	2010	500	$18.50	$9,250.00
P	X2222	X20400	T180	0400	A001	$0.00	1Q'10	2010	10000	$1.30	$13,000.00
P	X2907	X20600	CS	0600	S001	$0.00	1Q'10	2010	50	$9.20	$460.00
P	X3705	X24500	CS	4500	S001	$0.00	1Q'10	2010	50	$9.42	$471.00
P	X9702	X29702	T390	9702	G001	$5,123.39	1Q'10	2010	370	$276.94	$102,467.80
P	X2222	X20400	T180	0400	C002	$172.50	1Q'10	2010	100	$10.25	$1,025.00
P	X2222	X20400	T180	0400	R001	$0.00	1Q'10	2010	4000	$3.75	$15,000.00
P	X29700	X209700	T390	9700	A001	$0.00	1Q'10	2010	200	$5.89	$1,178.00
P	X8085	X28085	LC3	8085	H001	$0.00	1Q'10	2010	60	$9.83	$589.80
P Total											$268,441.60
S	LEAD FINISH	Charge	Charge	Charge	G001	$5,123.39	1Q'10	2010	370	$0.00	$0.00
S	SPECIAL TEST	Charge	Charge	Charge	C002	$172.50	1Q'10	2010	1	$1,500.00	$1,500.00
S	CD DATA DISK	Charge	Charge	Charge	C002	$172.50	1Q'10	2010	1	$925.00	$925.00
S	CD DATA DISK	Charge	Charge	Charge	R001	$0.00	1Q'10	2010	1	$1,000.00	$1,000.00
S	SPECIAL TEST	Charge	Charge	Charge	R001	$0.00	1Q'10	2010	1	$500.00	$500.00
S Total											$3,925.00
Grand Total											$301,029.60
	Note: This sample does not incorporate the actual database										

Subtotal Summary by Revenue Type

Revenue Type	Revenue	% Revenue
N	$28,663.00	9.5%
P	$268,441.60	89.2%
S	$3,925.00	1.3%
Total	$301,029.60	100.0%

Because the Revenue Types N and S have been determined to be both profitable and minor to the manufactured Product Revenue Type, these two Revenue Types will be ignored. The revised Simulation Spreadsheet is reduced to the Product Revenue only.

Product Revenue Spreadsheet

Revenue Type	Part Number	Part Description	Package Type	Die Geometry	Customer Group	Commission Amount	GL Quarter	GL Year	QTY	Unit Price	Revenue
P	X2907	X20600	T180	0600	A001	$0.00	1Q'10	2010	25000	$1.30	$32,500.00
P	X2907	X20600	T720	0006	A001	$0.00	1Q'10	2010	1000	$22.50	$22,500.00
P	X3507	X21506	T390	1506	A001	$0.00	1Q'10	2010	500	$6.00	$3,000.00
P	X3735	X20806	T390	0806	A001	$0.00	1Q'10	2010	1000	$4.80	$4,800.00
P	X3700	X24500	CS	4500	A001	$0.00	1Q'10	2010	1000	$7.00	$7,000.00
P	X2857	X20011	TY720	0011	A001	$0.00	1Q'10	2010	1000	$18.50	$18,500.00
P	X0918	X20003	T720	0003	A001	$0.00	1Q'10	2010	100	$13.50	$1,350.00
P	X2222	X20400	T180	0400	A001	$0.00	1Q'10	2010	2000	$4.75	$9,500.00
P	X3506	X21506	T390	1506	A001	$0.00	1Q'10	2010	500	$6.00	$3,000.00
P	X3700	X24500	T180	4500	A001	$0.00	1Q'10	2010	2000	$2.80	$5,600.00
P	X4261	X20014	T720	0014	A001	$0.00	1Q'10	2010	1000	$17.25	$17,250.00
P	X5109	X21009	T390	1009	A001	$0.00	1Q'10	2010	500	$18.50	$9,250.00
P	X2222	X20400	T180	0400	A001	$0.00	1Q'10	2010	10000	$1.30	$13,000.00
P	X2907	X20600	CS	0600	S001	$0.00	1Q'10	2010	50	$9.20	$460.00
P	X3705	X24500	CS	4500	S001	$0.00	1Q'10	2010	50	$9.42	$471.00
P	X9702	X29702	T390	9702	G001	$5,123.39	1Q'10	2010	370	$276.94	$102,467.80
P	X2222	X20400	T180	0400	C002	$172.50	1Q'10	2010	100	$10.25	$1,025.00
P	X2222	X20400	T180	0400	R001	$0.00	1Q'10	2010	4000	$3.75	$15,000.00
P	X29700	X209700	T390	9700	A001	$0.00	1Q'10	2010	200	$5.89	$1,178.00
P	X8085	X28085	LC3	8085	H001	$0.00	1Q'10	2010	60	$9.83	$589.80
P Total											$268,441.60

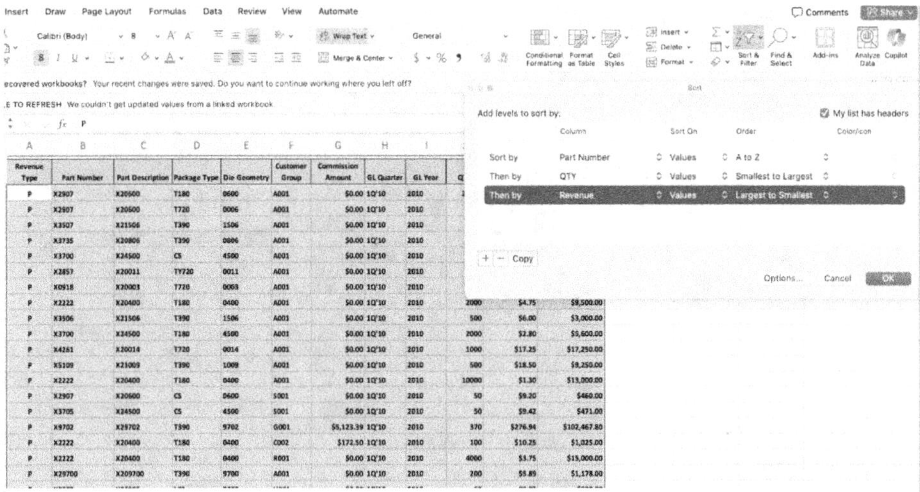

Excel Demonstration for Sorting by Item Number, Qty and Revenue

Sorted by Item Number, Qty and Revenue

Revenue Type	Part Number	Part Description	Package Type	Die Geometry	Customer Group	Commission Amount	GL Quarter	GL Year	QTY	Unit Price	Revenue
P	X0918	X20003	T720	0003	A001	$0.00	1Q'10	2010	100	$13.50	$1,350.00
P	X2222	X20400	T180	0400	A001	$0.00	1Q'10	2010	2000	$4.75	$9,500.00
P	X2222	X20400	T180	0400	A001	$0.00	1Q'10	2010	10000	$1.30	$13,000.00
P	X2222	X20400	T180	0400	C002	$172.50	1Q'10	2010	100	$10.25	$1,025.00
P	X2222	X20400	T180	0400	R001	$0.00	1Q'10	2010	4000	$3.75	$15,000.00
P	X2857	X20011	TY720	0011	A001	$0.00	1Q'10	2010	1000	$18.50	$18,500.00
P	X2907	X20600	T180	0600	A001	$0.00	1Q'10	2010	25000	$1.30	$32,500.00
P	X2907	X20600	T720	0006	A001	$0.00	1Q'10	2010	1000	$22.50	$22,500.00
P	X2907	X20600	CS	0600	S001	$0.00	1Q'10	2010	50	$9.20	$460.00
P	X29700	X209700	T390	9700	A001	$0.00	1Q'10	2010	200	$5.89	$1,178.00
P	X3506	X21506	T390	1506	A001	$0.00	1Q'10	2010	500	$6.00	$3,000.00
P	X3507	X21506	T390	1506	A001	$0.00	1Q'10	2010	500	$6.00	$3,000.00
P	X3700	X24500	CS	4500	A001	$0.00	1Q'10	2010	1000	$7.00	$7,000.00
P	X3700	X24500	T180	4500	A001	$0.00	1Q'10	2010	2000	$2.80	$5,600.00
P	X3705	X24500	CS	4500	S001	$0.00	1Q'10	2010	50	$9.42	$471.00
P	X3735	X20806	T390	0806	A001	$0.00	1Q'10	2010	1000	$4.80	$4,800.00
P	X4261	X20014	T720	0014	A001	$0.00	1Q'10	2010	1000	$17.25	$17,250.00
P	X5109	X21009	T390	1009	A001	$0.00	1Q'10	2010	500	$18.50	$9,250.00
P	X8085	X28085	LC3	8085	H001	$0.00	1Q'10	2010	60	$9.83	$589.80
P	X9702	X29702	T390	9702	G001	$5,123.39	1Q'10	2010	370	$276.94	$102,467.80
	Note: Sort by Item Number										

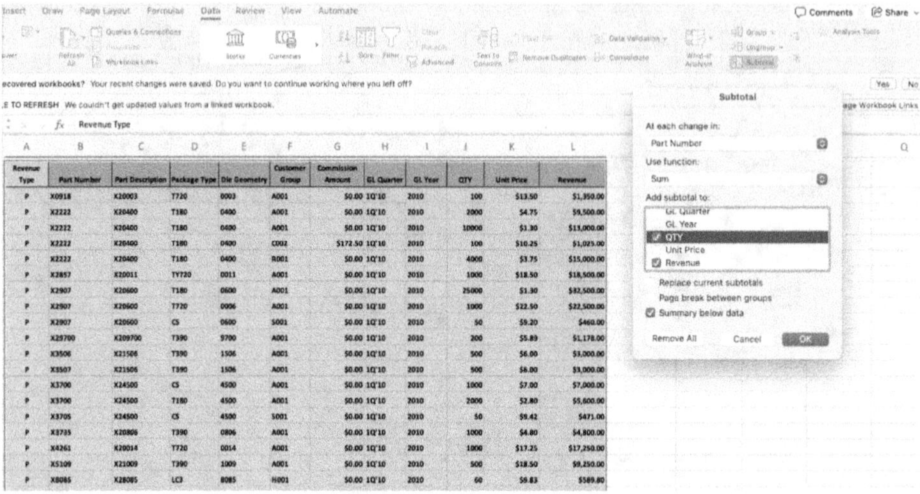

By subtotaling the Part Number, Qty and Revenue, the information necessary to provide the item (part) numbers contributing to Revenue and the level of quantity needed to satisfy these orders can be assessed.

It is important to know the parts (item types) most in demand and their relative contribution to revenue along with identifying what economies-of-scale at in play for the manufacturing entity.

Revenue Type	Part Number	Part Description	Package Type	Die Geometry	Customer Group	Commission Amount	GL Quarter	GL Year	QTY	Unit Price	Revenue
P	X0918	X20003	T720	0003	A001	$0.00	1Q'10	2010	100	$13.50	$1,350.00
	X0918 Total								100		$1,350.00
P	X2222	X20400	T180	0400	A001	$0.00	1Q'10	2010	2000	$4.75	$9,500.00
P	X2222	X20400	T180	0400	A001	$0.00	1Q'10	2010	10000	$1.30	$13,000.00
P	X2222	X20400	T180	0400	C002	$172.50	1Q'10	2010	100	$10.25	$1,025.00
P	X2222	X20400	T180	0400	R001	$0.00	1Q'10	2010	4000	$3.75	$15,000.00
	X2222 Total								16100		$38,525.00
P	X2857	X20011	TY720	0011	A001	$0.00	1Q'10	2010	1000	$18.50	$18,500.00
	X2857 Total								1000		$18,500.00
P	X2907	X20600	T180	0600	A001	$0.00	1Q'10	2010	25000	$1.30	$32,500.00
P	X2907	X20600	T720	0006	A001	$0.00	1Q'10	2010	1000	$22.50	$22,500.00
P	X2907	X20600	CS	0600	S001	$0.00	1Q'10	2010	50	$9.20	$460.00
	X2907 Total								26050		$55,460.00
P	X29700	X209700	T390	9700	A001	$0.00	1Q'10	2010	200	$5.89	$1,178.00
	X29700 Total								200		$1,178.00
P	X3506	X21506	T390	1506	A001	$0.00	1Q'10	2010	500	$6.00	$3,000.00
	X3506 Total								500		$3,000.00
P	X3507	X21506	T390	1506	A001	$0.00	1Q'10	2010	500	$6.00	$3,000.00
	X3507 Total								500		$3,000.00
P	X3700	X24500	CS	4500	A001	$0.00	1Q'10	2010	1000	$7.00	$7,000.00
P	X3700	X24500	T180	4500	A001	$0.00	1Q'10	2010	2000	$2.80	$5,600.00
	X3700 Total								3000		$12,600.00
P	X3705	X24500	CS	4500	S001	$0.00	1Q'10	2010	50	$9.42	$471.00
	X3705 Total								50		$471.00
P	X3735	X20806	T390	0806	A001	$0.00	1Q'10	2010	1000	$4.80	$4,800.00
	X3735 Total								1000		$4,800.00
P	X4261	X20014	T720	0014	A001	$0.00	1Q'10	2010	1000	$17.25	$17,250.00
	X4261 Total								1000		$17,250.00
P	X5109	X21009	T390	1009	A001	$0.00	1Q'10	2010	500	$18.50	$9,250.00
	X5109 Total								500		$9,250.00
P	X8085	X28085	LC3	8085	H001	$0.00	1Q'10	2010	60	$9.83	$589.80
	X8085 Total								60		$589.80
P	X9702	X29702	T390	9702	G001	$5,123.39	1Q'10	2010	370	$276.94	$102,467.80
	X9702 Total								370		$102,467.80
	Grand Total								50430		$268,441.60

To further simplify the analysis, isolate the subtotals.

Revenue Type	Part Number	Part Description	Package Type	Die Geometry	Customer Group	Commission Amount	GL Quarter	GL Year	QTY	Unit Price	Revenue
	X0918 Total								100		$1,350.00
	X2222 Total								16100		$38,525.00
	X2857 Total								1000		$18,500.00
	X2907 Total								26050		$55,460.00
	X29700 Total								200		$1,178.00
	X3506 Total								500		$3,000.00
	X3507 Total								500		$3,000.00
	X3700 Total								3000		$12,600.00
	X3705 Total								50		$471.00
	X3735 Total								1000		$4,800.00
	X4261 Total								1000		$17,250.00
	X5109 Total								500		$9,250.00
	X8085 Total								60		$589.80
	X9702 Total								370		$102,467.80
	Grand Total								50430		$268,441.60

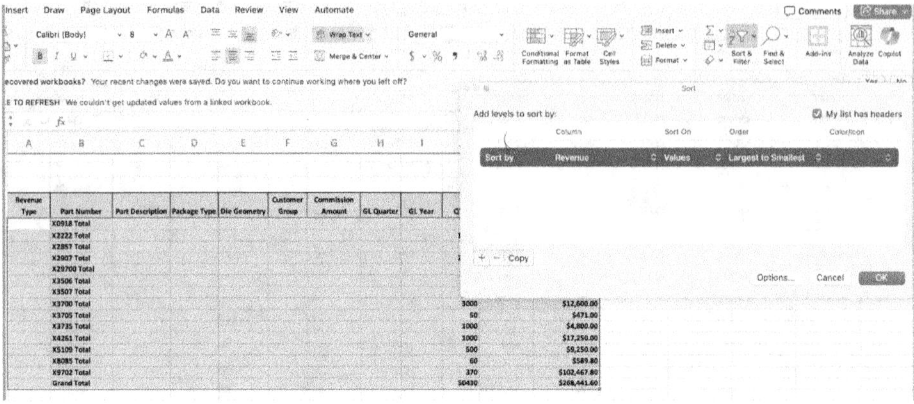

This sort for Revenue (largest-to-smallest) provides the first indication of the contribution to total revenue by Part Number and quantity of units sold under that part number. The other columns are no longer needed and are then eliminated for simplification. Additional columns are added to reflect: Accumulated Quantity, Accumulated Revenue, % Total Revenue, % cumulative Revenue, Line Items, % Line Items and ASP (Average Selling Price).

Part Number	QTY	Revenue	Accum. Qty	Accumulated Revenue	% Total Revenue	% Cumulative Revenue	line Items	% Line Items	ASP*
X9702 Total	370	$102,467.80	370	$102,467.80	38.2%	38.2%			
X2907 Total	26050	$55,460.00	26,420	$157,927.80	20.7%	58.8%			
X2222 Total	16100	$38,525.00	42,520	$196,452.80	14.4%	73.2%			
X2857 Total	1000	$18,500.00	43,520	$214,952.80	6.9%	80.1%	4	28.6%	$4.94
X4261 Total	1000	$17,250.00	44,520	$232,202.80	6.4%	86.5%	1	7.1%	
X3700 Total	3000	$12,600.00	47,520	$244,802.80	4.7%	91.2%	1	7.1%	$142.53
X5109 Total	500	$9,250.00	48,020	$254,052.80	3.4%	94.6%			
X3735 Total	1000	$4,800.00	49,020	$258,852.80	1.8%	96.4%	2	14.3%	$9.37
X3506 Total	500	$3,000.00	49,520	$261,852.80	1.1%	97.5%			
X3507 Total	500	$3,000.00	50,020	$264,852.80	1.1%	98.7%			
X0918 Total	100	$1,350.00	50,120	$266,202.80	0.5%	99.2%			
X29700 Total	200	$1,178.00	50,320	$267,380.80	0.4%	99.6%			
X8085 Total	60	$589.80	50,380	$267,970.60	0.2%	99.8%			
X3705 Total	50	$471.00	50,430	$268,441.60	0.2%	100.0%	6	42.9%	$6.80
Grand Total	50430	$268,441.60					14	100.0%	$5.32

***ASP: Average Sales Price**

Summary of Table Data for Charting

Revenue Level	80% Revenue	>80% to 90% Revenue	>90% to 95% Revenue	>95% to 100% Revenue	Totals
Revenue	$ 37,031,899	$ 4,581,698	$ 2,330,145	$ 2,327,049	$ 46,250,852
Part Numbers	4	1	1	2	14
% Part Numbers	28.60%	7.10%	7.10%	64.20%	100%
Total Units	43,520	1,000	3,000	1,500	50,430
ASP*	$4.94	$17.25	$4.20	$9.37	$9.08
Averaga Qty	10,880	1,000	3,000	750	3,602
* ASP: Average Sales Price					

Chart of Summary Data

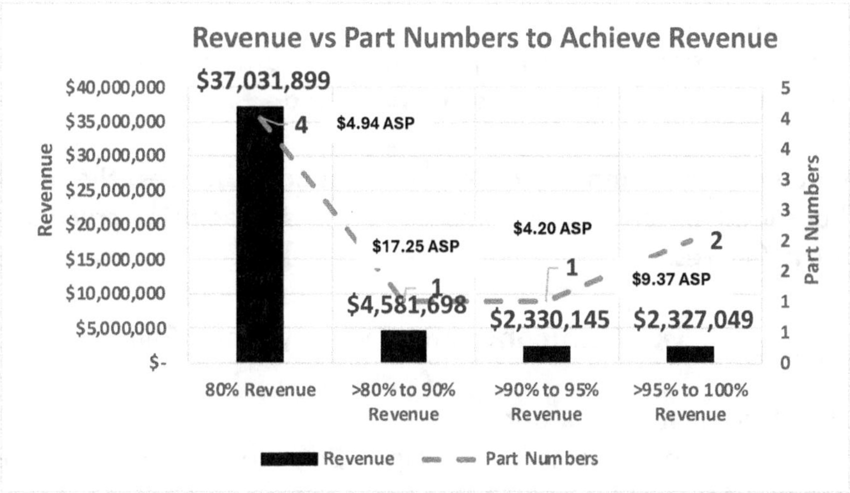

Simulation Sample Complete

Chapter 4

Semiconductor "Wire Creep" Failure

Overview

The problem presented in this chapter represents the use of all the documentation tools described in the Introduction. It will also enlist a significant efficiency step to facilitate resolution. This is an example where "time-is-money" was very important.

There was a significant amount anecdotal history but nothing solid from which to determine a cause for the failure mode that had existed in the commercial semiconductor industry off-and-on for over ten years.

How to approach a largely anecdotal set of data to determine what drives the root source of the problem is demonstrated.

Although this example involves semiconductor devices, the investigative methods used are broadly applicable to any manufacturing process involving reliability failures.

D0: Semiconductor "Wire Creep" Failure

D1: Select the Investigator(s)

Harry K. James, Plastic Package Engineering Manager, Principal Investigator/Analyst

D2: Describe the Problem

<u>What:</u> For more than ten years, the commercial semiconductor industry was plagued by the occurrence of integrated circuit semiconductor "wire creep' failures in applications not clearly defined by their occurrence.

Where: A specific failure rate and failure mode was noted by a customer whose application was "under-the-hood" electronic controls for motor vehicles.

When: During customer temperature cycle life testing of the motor vehicle application.

Who: A key industry wide customer who demanded resolution or disqualification of future across-the-board procurement.

How Big: Yearly Sales totaled approximately $10 million. (In today's financial environment, this would be more than $100 million).

Additional Information and Recorded Observations;

The wire creep failure is characterized by a break along slip planes or a fracture at grain boundaries; it is most frequently observed in thermal cycling reliability stress tests (Fig.1 and 2). This failure mechanism was widely identified in the early 1970s and persisted for more than a decade. Many attempts to solve this problem were published over the years.

Figure 1: A typical grain growth, "wire creep" failure

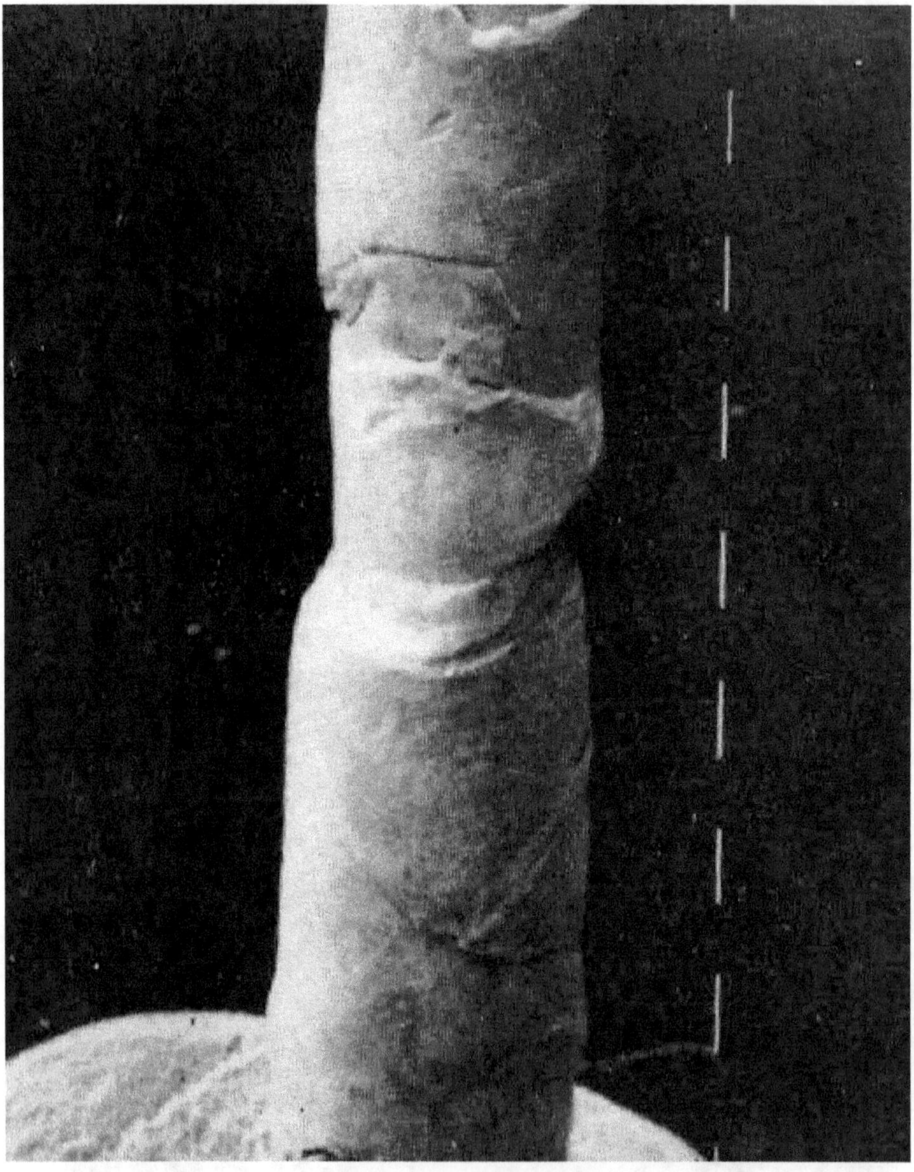

Figure 2: A typical example of advanced grain growth leading to complete wire failure

Over this decade-long period, periodic excursions in reliability performance tests, particularly temperature cycle stress testing, refocused attention throughout the industry but lost focus to resolve root cause when the problem appeared to subside from occurrence.

The manufacturing process begins with a singulated wafer-processed chip/die metallurgically attached to a selectively gold-plated Alloy 42 multiple device lead-frame (usually 10-up) which is then wire bonded for electronic connection, encapsulated with epoxy transfer molded plastic and finally trimmed and formed into final individual devices for testing.

The Problem Statement:

What is the inherent cause for failure only seen when commercial plastic encapsulated semiconductor transistor-transistor-logic (TTL) devices are subjected to temperature cycling under "bias" (electronically operating condition).

This prompts an Ishikawa "Fish Bone" Analysis aid for focus.

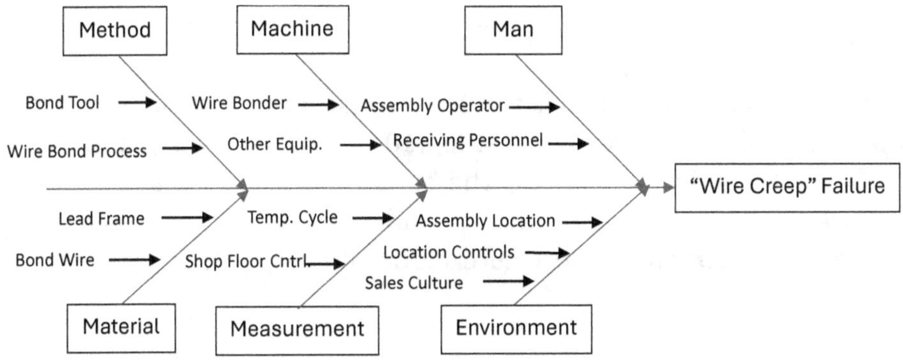

D3: Develop Interim Containment Actions

No interim mitigation was established because no existing test process could assure compliance to the customer application. Time was of the essence to determine and correct root cause and retain the customer.

D4: Determine and Verify Root Causes

From the Ishikawa "Fish Bone" diagram, a review is conducted to assess the ranking importance to the items listed as potential cause for the failure. Initial causal analysis focused on thermal and mechanical stresses imposed on the plastic encapsulated packaging system by materials and processes typically used in microdevice electronic device manufacturing.

Man:

Assembly operators were industry-level trained. The equipment they used was heavily mechanized, not automated, but easily set up and then monitored. There was no evidence of training procedure being compromised over this same long time period. The same can be said of the receiving personnel who accepted supplier materials. This failure mode was observed over almost a decade and was not isolated to any one manufacturer.

Machine:

The wire bonder used was an industry standard that had no history of causing any industry-wide failure modes. Other equipment in the assembly process had no direct link to the failure mode.

Method:

The manufacturing process is a batch process. Parts in a cassette with lead-frame strips of ten devices per strip (10-up) move as a group from one manufacturing station to another. The bond tools and mechanized wire bond process was well established within the industry and did not lend itself to any perceived contribution to the failure mode. Processes that were considered possible causes were:

1. Chip (die) attach heater block temperature
2. Wire bond (interconnection) capillary (through which wire passed to facilitate wire attachment) temperature
3. Bond wire tension

4. Wire bond dwell time (length of time taken to complete metallurgical attachment)
5. 1St bond force (at the chip bonding pad)
6. 2nd bond force (at the lead frame bonding pad)
7. Vibrational scrub time (dwell time vibrational time at 60 cycles per second)
8. Post transfer mold encapsulation cure temperature and time
9. Post package symbol marking cure temperature and time

Material:

The materials used in this operation were available from multiple sources in an established industry-wide supply chain. The materials used in this process were targeted for analysis as part of the experimental plan preparation.

1. Lead frame plating (supplier source)
2. Capillary type (metal or ceramic)
3. Gold wire type (manual or auto-bonder (AB))
4. Flame-off technique (to create a new ball at the end of the wire in preparation for the next wire bond cycle, Hydrogen gas or electronic (EFO).

Measurement:

For this specific customer application, temperature cycle produced this failure mode. Prior history for "Wire Creep" failure was observed industry-wide for over a decade but not at a level sufficient to isolate applications under which these devices were used and tested. The frequency of industry occurrence was "bothersome" but not critical. Commercial semiconductor devices are generally not designed into applications for which there are temperature excursions from ambient room temperature. Temperature control is normally a controlled parameter in commercial applications.

Temperature cycling is a slow process, one in which parts are moved from one temperature chamber at the low temperature to another at the high temperature. Industry standards required the part to be in a chamber temperature for a minimum of five (5) minutes and moved between chambers within one (1) minute. It was determined that the failure frequency could be replicated using thermal shock testing with perfluorocarbon liquid-to-liquid chambers with minimum dwell time of two (2) minutes and transfer time of ten (10) seconds. This represented significant test efficiency gain.

Environment:

Because this was an industry-wide problem, there was no evidence of assembly location or assembly controls contributing to this failure mode.

Semiconductor Device Construction

Let's take a moment to detail how a plastic encapsulated semiconductor integrated circuit is constructed.

Circuit components are constructed for mechanized assembly. At the time of this problem full automation for semiconductor assembly was not generally available. Mechanization was done using common carriers (a cassette) for the components to move from one mechanized assembly station to the next.

The lead frames used by the commercial semiconductor industry were procured from several different suppliers to the industry.

The lead frames were produced by progressive stamping on a reel-to-reel stamping machine. The stamped reel was then moved to a plating line where selective locations on the lead frame were plated with gold to facilitate die/chip attach and wire bonding by the semiconductor manufacturer. The lead frames were delivered to the manufacturer in strips of ten circuits per strip (10-up) and were presented with multiple strips per cassette to the assembly equipment.

The assembly sequence was (1) die/chip attach using mechanized pick-and-place equipment to attach the die/chip to the lead frame pad metallurgically, (2) advancing to mechanized wire bonding where thermocompression wire bonding completed for all bond wires, (3) then moved to a transfer molding machine where the devices were encapsulated in epoxy molding compound, finally (4) the 10-up stripes were the trimmed and formed for insertion to plastic tubes for presentation to mechanized test machines.

Figure 1 shows a single circuit cut from a 10-up strip as an example of the lead frame configuration. The shaded areas are those areas selective plated with gold for die/chip attach and wire bonding.

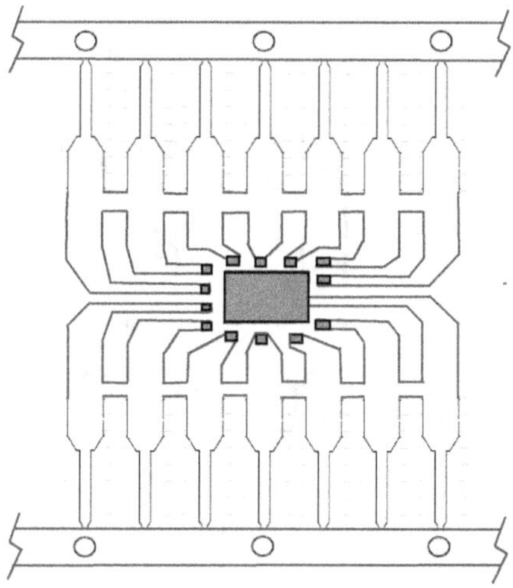

Figure 1: Single Circuit cut from 10-up Strip

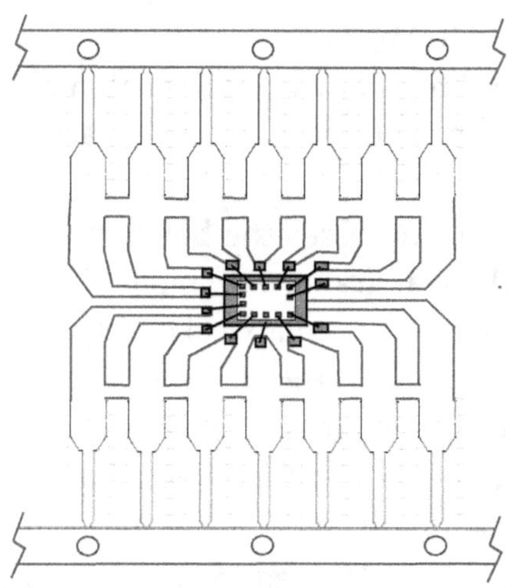

Figure 2: Lead Frame with Die/Chip attached and wire bonded.

For this semiconductor device, a thermocompression ball bond process uses a gold wire attached to aluminum pads on the die/chip and gold pad selective s on the lead frame. The steps are as follows:

1. A gold wire passes through a metal or ceramic bond capillary (Shown in cross section, Figure 3).

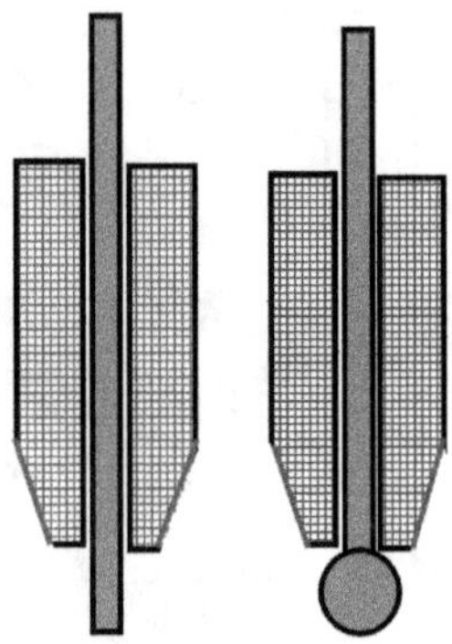

Figure 3: Cross section of capillary with unformed wire and formed wire for bonding.

2. A hydrogen torch or high voltage probe (EFO) pivots across the short wire extended from the capillary and melts the gold to reform as a ball at the end of the wire.
3. The bond tool moves to a position above the required die/chip bond pad using pattern recognition to accurately locate the die/chip bond pad.
4. The tool compresses the ball with a specified force against the die/chip pad. The lead frame die/chip pad is heated sufficiently to allow the die/chip to form a metallurgical bond.
5. The programmed tool then moves to the lead frame bond pad where the bond compression applied force and heat energy between the capillary tip and the pad form the metallurgical connection between the wire and the lead frame pad.
6. With the wire clamped to prevent movement, the wire is pulled form the lead frame pad creating a “stitch” bond. A small tail of the wire

is programmed to extend from the end of the capillary, and the next cycle begins by forming a new ball.

Figure 4: Sketch shows wire bond profile die/chip to lead frame.

Figure 5 shows the device after molding encapsulation and trim-and-form operations.

Figure 5: Finished Dual-in-Line Plastic Encapsulated Packaged Device

Initial Test Matrix

The nine methods variables and the four materials variables were combined for an initial test.

Table 1: Plastic Package Assembly Variables and Relative Influence on Wire Creep and Grain Growth Failure

Influence of Variables	Experimental Variable
Minor Influence	Heater Block Temperature Capillary Temperature Wire Tension Dwell tIME 1st bond force 2nd bond force Vibrational scrub Post mold cure Top symbol cure
Major influence	Lead frame plating Capillary Type Gold wire type Flame-off

Two groups of parts were assembled, one group under standard assembly conditions and materials (the control group) and a second group under adjusted experimental conditions. These adjusted conditions were based on a review of the conditions that were adjusted to reduce thermal and mechanical stress.

The results of the thermal shock stress test showed the classical failure rate for the control group; that is, 30% cumulative failure at 250 cycles, 75% cumulative failure at 500 cycles and 98% cumulative failure at 750 cycles. For the experimental group, there were zero failures at 1,000 cycles. Thus, the first goal – fixing the problem – was achieved.

To identify the true contributors to the success of the trial group, a two-level, full factorial test matrix would be required. For thirteen variables, this would mean a test matrix of 2^{13} (8,192) elements, with each element requiring fifty devices for testing. This was not a practical task, given cost/benefit consideration.

From Table 2, reconsideration centered on the fact that several of the individual variable adjustments were detrimental to established productivity levels. Based on this consideration, the nine process variables were returned to their original standard value. The remaining four materials variable were subjected to a two-level, full factorial analysis.

Test groups were assembled, one with the control group materials and the remaining fifteen groups with each of the four materials choices (sixteen groups of four each, 2^4). The results are shown in Table 2.

Table 2: Wire Creep, Grain Growth Major Contributor Test Matrix and Stress Test Results

Run	Leadframe	Capillary	Gold Wire	Flame-off	250	500	750	1000
1	Vendor "A"	Metal	AB	EFO	4/50	2/46	21 /44	1 /23
2	Vendor "A"	Metal	AB	H_2	23/50	4/27	21/23	1 /2
3	Vendor "A"	Metal	Manual	EFO	8/50	1/42	29/41	4/12
4	Vendor "A"	Metal	Manual	H_2	18/50	3/32	25/29	2/4
5	Vendor "A"	Ceramic	AB	EFO	1/50	0/49	3/49	0/46
6	Vendor "A"	Ceramic	AB	H_2	17/50	2/33	29/ 31	0/2
7	Vendor "A"	Ceramic	Manual	EFO	5/50	3/45	5/42	6/37
8	Vendor "A"	Ceramic	Manual	H_2	3/50	0/47	30/47	9/17
9	In-House	Metal	AB	EFO	0/50	2/50	0/48	0/48
10	In-House	Metal	AB	H_2	0/50	3/50	2/47	9/45
11	In-House	Metal	Manual	EFO	1/50	0/49	0/49	3/49
12	In-House	Metal	Manual	H_2	0/50	1f50	9/49	21/40
13	In-House	Ceramic	AB	EFO	O/50	O/50	0/50	0/50
14	In-House	Ceramic	AB	H_2	1 /50	1 /49	5/48	16/43
15	In-House	Ceramic	Manual	EFO	1 /50	0/49	0/49	2/49
16	In-House	Ceramic	Manual	H_2	0/50	0/50	2/50	15/48

The results confirm the irrelevance of the processing variables as potential causes for the device failures. More surprisingly, the results do not point to single cause for the observed failure but to four independent causes for the observed failure.

The four variables identified for full evaluation were (1) lead frame (a vendor plated lead frame versus an internally plated lead frame), (2) capillary type (metal versus ceramic), (3) gold wire type (manual versus modified auto bonding wire), and (4) flame-off ball formation technique (hydrogen torch versus electronic flame-off).

Again, a full two-level full factorial analysis was completed. Table 3 summarizes the results.

Table 3. Summary of Normalized Individual Variable Contribution to Wire Creep and Grain Growth Failures

	Thermal Shock Cycles			
Normailized Contributor Comparison	250	500	750	1000
Lead Frame				
In-house--platedlead frame failures	3	10	28	94
Vendor "A"--plateed lead frame failures	79	91	257	280
% Contribution	82	63	65	36
Falme-off				
EFO failures	20	28	86	102
Hydrogen failures	62	76	199	272
% Contribution	10	18	16	32
Capillary				
Ceramic failures	28	34	108	156
Metal failures	54	70	177	218
% Contribution	6	14	12	17
Wire				
Automatic bonder wire failures	46	60	141	168
Manual bonder wire failures	36	44	144	206
% Contribution	2	5	7	15

The first variable, lead frame, was notably unexpected.

Lead frames are a normal supply chain item in the semiconductor industry. Some early experience recorded a non-specific tendency for higher incidence of observed wire creep.

Figure 6 is a graphical presentation of the tabular data in Table III. There are several immediate conclusions that can be made from the chart.

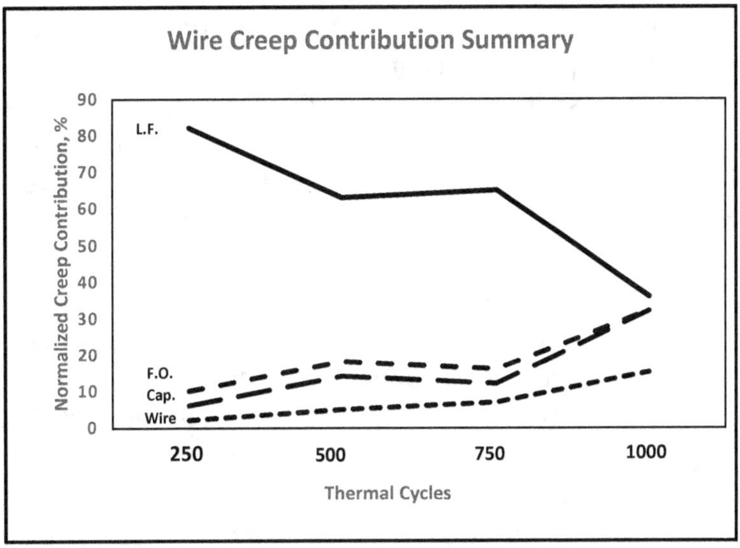

Figure 6: Graphical summary of normalized individual variable contribution to wire creep grain growth failure.

First, the Vendor "A" plated lead frame exerted significant accelerating influence on the failure rate. Second, the use of hydrogen torch flame-off ball formation always created wire creep failure. Third, the capillary type and wire type contributed significantly less to the failure rate than the first two variables but were nonetheless significant.

It was suspected that a contaminant was present on the lead frame. Using electron spectroscopy for chemical analysis (ESCA) it was determined after several attempts at different beam energies that Thallium was detected essentially as a monolayer on the surface of the gold plating. Further, understanding for this resulted from the fact that gold electroplaters commonly used Thallium sulfate as a grain refiner. The Thallium was co-deposited during the electroplating operation.

It was necessary to determine how the Thallium found its way to the area above the ball bond and to explain, metallurgically, how Thallium caused the grain growth and accelerated failure.

It was hypothesized that during the "stitch bond" operation on the lead frame gold bonding pad (connecting the semiconductor chip to the external world through the lead frame), the gold wire became contaminated by contact to the high Thallium content gold of the lead frame. Upon recrystallization of the gold wire tail to form a new gold ball at the end of the wire, the Thallium was dispersed throughout the wire and migrated rapidly along the wire.

To prove this transport hypothesis, it was necessary to collect a large number of gold balls to a sample of sufficient quantity to detect Thallium in the newly formed balls. Subsequently, Secondary Ion Mass Spectroscopy was able to detect significant levels of Thallium. At the high end of Thermal Shock, Condition C (150 °C), a molten gold-Thallium eutectic occurs. This eutectic melts between 131 °C and 142 °C allowing the eutectic to migrate to grain boundaries resulting in succeedingly weakened boundaries and ultimate open circuit failure over many temperature cycles.

The data supports the conclusion that hydrogen torch flame-off to create a new ball at the end of the gold bonding wire always results, in time, with wire creep failure. It was hypothesized that hydrogen may reduce the oxides of gold wire impurities and form trapped, insoluble water which nucleates and grows at grain boundaries during thermal temperature cycling. This hypothesis was judged to unjustified for proof by cost/benefit determination. Changing to electronic discharge ball formation was adopted to replace the hydrogen torch technique.

The metal capillary produced failure when a ceramic capillary did not. As a heat conductive material, the metal capillary can reach a much higher temperature than the ceramic, whose thermal conductivity is much less. With a metal capillary, the thermal effect on the wire is compounded by the fact that the wire moves through the heated capillary as it moves from the first ball bond on the chip to the stitch bond on the lead frame. Some of this wire moves through the capillary several times during repeated wire bonding operations. The metal capillary transfers heat more efficiently to the gold wire during recrystallization, expanding the range over which thermal, mechanical and metallurgical stress can be induced.

Finally, the bonding wire itself is a contributor to the wire creep failure. There were two main types of wire used in this study. Wire typically used for manual binding equipment (manual) and wire used for mechanized auto bonding equipment (AB) . The manual wire always produced failure when used with the mechanized bonding equipment. Several types of auto binding wire were evaluated, and while all auto bonding wire performed better than manual bond wire, it was determined that a specific formulation was superior. That final determination is detailed in Table 4. The result was that a reduction in the copper impurity (less than 1 ppm) and the inclusion of Beryllium (3.4 ppm) resulted in no failures.

Table 4. Gold Bonding Wire Thermal Shock Performance: Copper and Beryllium

Wire Constituents (ppm)					Results (failures) Thermal Shock, Condition C (cycles)											
Run	Cu	Ag	Si	Be	250	500	750	1000	1250	1500	1750	2000	2250	2500	2750	3000
1*	40	10	20	4	3/48	4/45	12/41	6/29	21/23	1/2	0/1	1/1	--	--	--	--
2**	25-50	10-30	5-10	8	0	0	0	0	2/50	1/48	0/47	0/47	4/47	2/43	0/41	0/41
3**	20-40	10-30	2-5	4.5	0	0	0	0	0	0	2/50	0/40	0/48	2/48	0/46	0/46
4**	<1	10-30	7-15	3.4	0	0	0	0	0	0	0	0	0	0	0	0

* Control: assembled with Thallium-contaminated lead frame, metal capillary, manual wire (25 um), and hydrogen flame-off.

** Experimental: Assembled with Thallium-free lead frame, ceramic capillary, experimental wire (25um AB-type) and EFO.

Notes:

(1) All other bonding conditions were identical

(2) All analyzed failures resulted from wire creep, grain growth.

To summarize, there were four independent root causes for this wire creep failure mode. The lead frame electroplating was the most accelerating and significant influence. The hydrogen flame-off was second to the lead frame and the metal capillary and the gold bonding wire metallurgical formulation were slightly less significant contributors to the failure mode.

D5: Choose and Validate Permanent Corrective Actions

Devices assembled with the best choices of materials (non-Thallium contaminated lead frame, electronic discharge formed gold ball, ceramic capillary and metallurgically reformulated gold bonding wire) resulted in the ability to withstand 3,000 thermal shock cycles with zero failures. (Recall that the original failure rate was 50% at a mere 250 thermal cycles).

D6: Implement Permanent Corrective Actions

Upon publication of this study, the semiconductor industry moved to adopt and implement all the corrective actions to eliminate this failure mode.

D7: Prevent Recurrence

There was no return to the use of the materials that contributed to this failure mode.

D8: Recognize Team and Individuals

An honorarium was presented to the investigator for this work.

Afterthoughts

Commercial semiconductors are not typically used in extreme temperature applications. Commercial semiconductors are usually found in controlled environments where heat is removed by conduction (metal heat sinks) or air convection (fans). The application here was automobile engine compartment electronic control which has a wide window of operating temperature exposure. Acceptance testing for commercial semiconductors does not typically include temperature cycle testing.

In the military, aerospace and space semiconductor segment, 100% temperature cycle testing is a required acceptance test.

Automotive manufacturers do not want to incur the cost for these types of high reliability devices. The chip/die packaged in a military, aerospace or space qualified package for a HiRel application is far more costly to produce and test than that packaged for commercial use.

This study was forced to resolution by leverage: money. Find the cause, correct it or lose the customer and its revenue – permanently.

A chief fear throughout the semiconductor industry, and other industries, as well, is the fear of latent failure modes. These are failure modes that are undetected during processing or in acceptance testing for shipment. A field failure of this type draws attention that is clearly unfavorable to the manufacturer who supplied the part. It can severely impact revenue and reputation.

The types of devices described in this study were produced in production volumes of a million per day by multiple semiconductor manufacturers using these same processing materials. Only when subjected to temperature cycling was this failure mode realized. There were multiple lead frame suppliers to this industry. Some used Thallium sulfate in the selective gold plating and some did not. It is unknown even statistically but is likely that, for more than a decade, there were many devices sold throughout the semiconductor customer base with this latent failure mode. As long as system operating temperature was close to ambient room temperature using heat sinking techniques or internal electronic system cooling fans, this failure mode was never observed, at least not at an industry reporting level.

The semiconductor industry is constantly looking to improve performance and cost. To that end, the assembly materials identified in this study were completely changed to meet this benefit. By the late 1980s, the assembly process was changed from Alloy 42 gold spot-plated lead frame with eutectic die attach and thermocompression gold ball bonding to copper 194 lead frame with silver spot-plated lead frame and silver flake filled epoxy die attach and ultrasonic aluminum wire bonding.

This construction change facilitated better thermal dissipation characteristics with less temperature stress-induced processing techniques and lower costs.

While there was no explicit statement, this task was assigned with a clearly implied understanding that failure to find the cause and take corrective action would likely have serious career consequences. It was clear that the upper-level business management was pleased that a source of significant revenue was retained and the defamation from disqualification from future business was avoided. What stood out more personally was the peer level accolades for how the study was carried out. It was considered a benchmark in successful methodology.

This example presents both deductive and inductive solutions to the problem. The lead frame and the bonding wire were deductively determined with objective measurements and data. The bonding capillary and hydrogen torch causes were assessed using inductive analysis in the absence of objective data.

Validation was achieved when no failures were observed on the same quantity of devices as used in each of the trials to resolve the problem after 3,000 thermal shock tests.

A resolved problem may have more than one cause.

Chapter 4 Bibliography

"Metallurgical Behavior of Gold Wire in Thermal Compression Bonding" by T. H. Ramsey, Solid State Technology, October 1973, pp. 43-47.

"Bonding Wire Failure Mode in Plastic Encapsulated Integrated Circuits" by C. N. Adams, 11th Annual Proceedings IEEE Reliability Physics Symposium, 1973, pp. 41-44.

"Metallurgical Failure Modes of Wire Bonds" by G. G. Harmon, 12th Annual Proceedings IEEE Reliability Physics Symposium, 1974, pp. 131-141.

"Diffusion of Gold and Silver in Thallium" by J. R. Anthony, B. F Dyson and D. Turnbull, Journal of Applied Physics, February 1968, pp. 1391-1395.

"Resolution of Gold Wire Grain Growth Failure Mechanism in Plastic Encapsulated Microelectronic Devices", by H. K. James, IEEE Transactions on Components, Hybrids, and Manufacturing Technology, Volume CHMT-3, No.3, September 1980, pp. 370-375.

"Resolution of Gold Wire Grain Growth Failure Mechanism" by Harry K. James, Semiconductor International, Vol. 3, No. 9, October 1980, pp. 95-111.

"Effects of Gold-Plating Additives on Semiconductor Wire Bonding" by Duane W. Endicott, Harry K. James and Fred Nobel, Plating and Surface Finishing, November 1981, pp. 58-61.

Chapter 5

Artificial Intelligence in Problem Resolution

Overview

Artificial Intelligence is not proposed for use; its use is mandatory. At the very least, it will be used for efficient reference work for problem resolution. It may potentially be used to solve a problem; that is yet to be demonstrated with any consistency. What it cannot do (yet) is carry out physical evaluations, experiments or conduct validation of problem resolution corrective action. Human intervention for validation is required. The use of AI is an example where "time-is-money" efficiency is critically important.

The author's input is reflected in this chapter by "Question/Response:". ChatGPT's response follows the author's question or response to ChatGPT in its native format.

How Does AI Work

AI simulates human intelligence in machines, enabling them to learn, reason, solve problems, perceive, and understand language to perform tasks. AI systems use algorithms to analyze large language data bases, to find hidden patterns, and learn from them.

OpenAI's ChatGPT doesn't "learn" or accumulate new information over time like a human does. Instead, its large language data base knowledge is static at the time of its training and doesn't update dynamically through interactions. However, OpenAI (and other AI chatbots) conducts several tests before releasing an updated version to measure and evaluate its performance and efficiency in processing information:

OpenAI benchmarks models on standardized datasets for reasoning, coding, and general knowledge. These benchmarks help compare the performance of different versions and measure improvements in understanding and problem resolution.

The correctness and relevance of an update's answers are evaluated by comparing responses to verified sources and expert judgments.

An updated model is evaluated against the current released model and earlier models based on reasoning speed, multimodal capabilities (handling text, images, and potentially audio), and how well it maintains context across conversations.

OpenAI updates models based on advances in AI research, including better training techniques, efficiency improvements, and new architectures. If vulnerabilities or harmful biases are detected, OpenAI may update or adjust how the model behaves.

An updated model is designed to generate responses faster and more efficiently than previous models. This means it can "reason" through problems in fewer computational steps, making it more efficient rather than "learning" in a traditional sense.

OpenAI collects feedback from users to refine future models. While the current released model itself doesn't update, feedback helps improve future iterations.

The following dialogue with ChatGPT illuminates a specific description of OpenAI's update from one model to the next. The dialogue was only slightly modified for grammatical clarification with no changes to substance presented.

Question/Response: What is the comparison between the current model and GPT 4/GPT 4o?

[This comparison and responses to subsequent queries was generated in this format by ChatGPT with minor text clarifications by the author.]

Here's the comparison of GPT-4 / GPT-4o vs newer models:

GPT-4 (2023 era)

- First strong "reasoning-capable" model.
- Good at:
    - structured thinking
    - technical explanation
- Limitations:
    - slower
    - weaker long-context handling
    - less natural dialogue

GPT-4o ("omni")

- Built for:
    - speed
    - multimodal (text, image, voice)
    - conversational feel

Key traits:

- Faster, more responsive.
- More personable / adaptive tone.
- Strong for:
    - general Q&A
    - creative tasks
    - conversational interaction

But:

- Slightly weaker in deep, multi-step reasoning
- Can be more "agreeable" or conversationally biased

In practice:

GPT-4o feels like a very capable assistant but not always a rigorous analytical partner

Newer generation (GPT-5-class)

Core shift:
From chat assistant → reasoning system.

Key differences that matter:

1. Reasoning depth

- GPT-4o: good
- Newer models: significantly stronger
- Better at:
    - multi-step logic
    - system modeling
    - hypothesis building

2. Accuracy & reliability

- Newer models:
    - fewer hallucinations
    - more careful framing
    - better distinction:
        - evidence vs inference

Measurable improvements in medical-style reasoning benchmarks (GPT-5)

3. Behavioral tone

- GPT-4o:
    - more conversational
    - sometimes overly agreeable
- Newer models:
    - more direct, analytical, less "flattering"
    - less likely to reinforce weak ideas
- When needed, pushback and structure, not validation

4. Complex synthesis
This is the biggest difference.
Newer models are much better at:

- integrating:
    - neuroscience
    - clinical reasoning
    - behavioral observations
- maintaining coherence across long, multi-session threads

5. Speed vs depth tradeoff

- GPT-4o:
    - faster
    - more fluid
- Newer models:
    - slightly slower
    - but deeper and more structured (Analytics Vidhya)

Simple comparison table

Capability	GPT-4	GPT-4o	Newer (GPT-5-class)
Speed	Medium	Fast	Medium
Conversational tone	Good	Excellent	Controlled / precise
Deep reasoning	Good	Moderate	Excellent
Long-context synthesis	Moderate	Good	Excellent
Clinical-style thinking	Moderate	Moderate	Strong
Reliability/hallucination	Moderate	Good	Best

Bottom line

- GPT-4o = Excellent conversational assistant.
- Newer model (like this) = analytical collaborator for complex reasoning.

Question/Response: What different models are there?

Think of models as tools, not "versions".

Different models are optimized for different types of work:

- reasoning
- speed
- coding
- conversation
- multimodal (images, audio)

Current major categories of models:

1. Reasoning-focused models
Purpose: Deep thinking, structured analysis, multi-step logic
Examples:

- GPT-5-class (current system)
- Earlier: GPT-4 (to a lesser extent)

Best for:

- Clinical hypothesis building
- Engineering analysis
- Complex problem resolution
- Long-form structured documents

2. Fast / conversational models
Purpose: Speed, fluid interaction, general use
Example:

- GPT-4o

Best for:

- Everyday questions
- Brainstorming
- Writing drafts
- Casual interaction

Tradeoff:

- Faster, but less rigorous reasoning

3. Coding / technical models
Purpose: Software development, debugging
Examples:

- Code-focused GPT variants
- Integrated IDE copilots

Best for:

- Writing code
- Debugging
- Technical documentation

4. Specialized / domain-tuned models

These are not always publicly labeled, but exist as:

- medical-tuned
- legal-tuned
- finance-tuned

They:

- follow stricter reasoning patterns
- are more conservative
- prioritize accuracy over creativity

5. Multimodal models

Purpose: Work across:

- text
- images
- audio
- video

Example:

- GPT-4o

Best for:

- analyzing images
- generating diagrams
- voice interaction

Another way to understand it:

Models differ along 3 axes:

1. Depth vs Speed

- Deep = reasoning models
- Fast = conversational models

2. Precision vs Creativity

- Precise = analytical models
- Creative = writing / ideation models

3. General vs Specialized

- General = GPT-4o
- Specialized = coding / domain models

Simple comparison

Model Type	Strength	Weakness
Reasoning (GPT-5-class)	Deep analysis	Slower
GPT-4o	Fast, natural	Less rigorous
Coding models	Technical precision	Narrow scope
Multimodal	Flexible inputs	Varies by task

One important caution:
Different models can:

- give different answers to the same question

Why?

- Different optimization goals
- Different reasoning depth

Bottom line

There isn't "one best model."
There are different tools for different cognitive tasks.

<u>Question/Response:</u> How are these models chosen when a query is presented?

1. How to tell which model you're using:
Most reliable way:
Look at the model label in the interface

- Usually shown at the top of the chat
- Or in a dropdown selector

Examples you might see:

- "GPT-4o"
- "GPT-5" / "Reasoning"
- "Auto"

That label is the ground truth

Behavioral clues (secondary, not perfect):

If the label isn't obvious, you can infer:

Reasoning model Structured answers

- Pushes back on weak ideas
- Distinguishes:
  - evidence vs inference
- Good at:
  - multi-step logic
  - long continuity

GPT-4o (fast model)

- Very quick responses
- More conversational
- More agreeable
- Less likely to challenge you

Simple rule:

If it feels like a thoughtful analyst, it's a reasoning model; if it feels like a fast assistant, it's GPT-4o.

2. How to deliberately choose a model:

This depends on your interface, but typically:

Method 1: Model selector (most common)
Look for:

- Dropdown at top of chat
- Button labeled something like:
    - "GPT-4o"
    - "Reasoning"
    - "Auto"

You can:

- Start a new chat
- Select the model you want

This is the cleanest way

Method 2: Start a new conversation
Model choice is usually set per conversation

So:

- New chat = new model selection opportunity

Method 3: "Auto mode" (important)
Some interfaces default to:

Auto

Meaning:

- System chooses model based on task
-

Tradeoff:

- Convenient
- But less predictable

Important constraints

1. You cannot switch models mid-thread (usually)

- Once a conversation starts:
    - model stays fixed

To change:

- start a new chat

2. Same question ≠ same answer across models

Different models:

- prioritize different things
- may give different conclusion

3. When YOU should choose which model:

When to use GPT-4o:

- Quick drafts
- Brainstorming
- Casual questions
- Writing tone adjustments

When to switch intentionally:

Task	Best Model
Deep analysis	Reasoning model
Fast answers	GPT-4o
Writing polish	GPT-4o
Technical modeling	Reasoning model

4. A simple workflow (very useful)

You can combine models:

Step 1:
Use reasoning model → build structure, logic

Step 2:

Switch to GPT-4o → polish wording, simplify

Final takeaway

- Check the label → that tells you the model
- Choose via dropdown → that controls it
- New chat = new choice

[End of ChatGPT dialogue]

Quality Assurance

Ensuring the safety of AI tools requires a comprehensive quality assurance (QA) scope that addresses various aspects of development, deployment, and usage. Here are key components that should be included in the QA scope for developing safe AI tools:

1. Compliance and Standards: Ensure compliance with industry standards, regulations, and best practices (e.g., ISO/IEC 27001 for information security, ISO/IEC 2382 for AI vocabulary). During development, clear safety requirements based on the intended use cases of the AI tool are defined.

2. Conduct thorough risk assessments to identify potential hazards associated with the AI tool. Develop and implement strategies to mitigate identified risks.

3. Ensure high-quality, accurate, and unbiased data is used for training and testing AI models. Implement measures to protect user data and ensure privacy compliance (e.g., General Data Protection Regulation (GDPR), European Union and California Consumer Protection Act (CCPA)).

4. Maintain transparency in model development, including documentation of model architecture, training data, and decision-making processes. Implement techniques to detect and mitigate biases in AI models. Ensure the AI tool provides explanations for its decisions, making it understandable to users and stakeholders.

5. Validate the functionality of the AI tool to ensure it performs as intended. Assess the performance, scalability, and efficiency of the AI tool. Test the AI tool under various scenarios and edge cases to ensure robustness. Safety Testing: Conduct specific tests to validate the safety features and fail-safes of the AI tool.

6. Ensure there is adequate human oversight (human-in-the-loop) in critical decision-making processes. Collect and incorporate user feedback to improve the AI tool's safety and usability.

7. Implement continuous monitoring of the AI tool's performance and behavior in real-world conditions. Develop and maintain incident response plans to address any safety issues that arise post-deployment. Regularly update the AI tool to address vulnerabilities, improve safety features, and enhance functionality.

8. Establish and adhere to ethical guidelines for AI development and deployment. Engage with stakeholders, including users, regulators, and ethicists, to ensure the AI tool aligns with societal values and norms.

9. Maintain detailed documentation of all aspects of the AI tool, including design, development, testing, and deployment processes. Publish transparency reports to provide insights into the AI tool's operation, performance, and safety measures.

10. Ensure the AI tool complies with relevant legal and regulatory requirements. Conduct third-party audits to validate the safety and compliance of the AI tool.

By encompassing these components, ChatGPT maintains that the QA scope for AI tools can ensure they are developed and deployed in a manner that prioritizes safety, reliability, and ethical considerations.

How to Work Around the Static Nature

Since AI's knowledge is static and does not update dynamically, users can enhance their experience and work around its limitations in several ways.

One can integrate real-time tools and external resources. For example, some platforms allow ChatGPT to access the internet for real-time data. If you need up-to-date news, stock prices, or other live information, you can manually verify facts using search engines.

Connecting AI to a structured database (via retrieval-augmented generation, or RAG) can provide more relevant and fresh responses.

The AI you are using may be able to integrate with custom Application Programming Interfaces (APIs) and third-party integrations that fetch live weather updates, sports scores, or financial market data.

If you need AI to remember previous responses, summarize key points and feed them back in each interaction. For example: "Previously, we discussed X and Y. Now, let's continue with Z." You can use notes and summaries stored in external memory to retain AI-generated insights and revisiting them as needed can help simulate "memory."

There are many more opportunities to use external resources if needed. Each AI model has online response capability to assist. These external tools can assist in various tasks, from drafting content and analyzing data to providing real-time information and maintaining privacy. Exploring them can help you determine which best fits your specific needs.

Optimizing Query Structure for Better Responses

Asking better-structured questions leads to more precise answers. Some techniques:

Be Specific & Context-Rich:
Instead of: "Tell me about climate change policies."
Try: "What are the key climate change policies introduced in the U.S. in 2023?"

Use Iterative Questioning:
If a response is too general, follow up with: "Can you expand on the economic impacts of those policies?"

Combining AI with Human Expertise:
ChatGPT-5.2 is Excellent for brainstorming, summarizing, and automating repetitive tasks, but human validation is essential when dealing with complex or high-stakes decisions.

Whenever an AI response is a stated position or conclusion, always ask for a list of published references that support the position or conclusion presented by AI. Moreover, when AI responds with a conclusive statement, always ask for the counter argument to the AI position or conclusion. As the investigator or team member attempting to resolve a problem, you are responsible for confirming the validity of the references that AI cites. AI is a virtual assistant; you are the arbiter of truth.

If the question or information you ask or request is better sourced from another chatbot, ChatGPT will request your permission to submit the question or request to the chatbot that it deems is more likely to provide a more substantial or accurate response.

The Most Common Uses for AI

Here are the top ten applications according to OpenAI.

1. Customer Support:
   - Automating responses to frequently asked questions.
   - Assisting with troubleshooting and providing solutions to common issues.

2. Content Creation:
   - Generating articles, blog posts, and social media content.
   - Assisting with scriptwriting and creative writing projects.

3. Education and Tutoring:
   - Providing explanations for complex topics.
   - Assisting with homework and studying by answering questions.

4. Personal Assistance:
   - Scheduling and reminders.
   - Managing emails and drafting responses.

5. Language Translation:
   - Translating text between different languages.
   - Offering real-time translation for communication.

6. Code Assistance:
   - Helping with coding problems and debugging.
   - Providing code snippets and explanations for programming concepts.

7. Market Research:
   - Analyzing market trends and summarizing research reports.
   - Generating insights from large datasets.

8. Healthcare Support:
   - Offering information on medical conditions and treatments.
   - Assisting with mental health support through conversation and resources.

9. Gaming and Entertainment:
   - Creating interactive storytelling experiences.

- Developing in-game dialogues and character interactions.

10. Legal Assistance:
   - Summarizing legal documents and cases.
   - Providing information on legal terms and processes.

Benefits

An AI tool such as OpenAI's ChatGPT can be used for reference. In the discussion of the Apollo Lunar Module RCS system for spacecraft attitude control (Chapter 1) the contract under which the U. S Bureau of Mines undertook to analyze the ignition problem observed in a space-level environment required a six-month literature search for relevant information upon which to base an experimental investigation.

At the time of this investigation, the internet and search engines did not exist.

The first two months were spent searching the local area and arranging with information retrieval agencies, such as the Chemical Propulsion information Agency, NASA Scientific and Information Facility, the library of Congress, the Science Information Exchange of the Smithsonian Institution and the Defense Documentation Center based on a "key word" list. The next few months were spent collecting hard copies for cataloging and review.

This was obviously time-intensive and staff-consuming. With today's search systems, these inquiries can significantly increase efficiency in reaching a problem resolution with only hours required rather than months and, likely, only one research person. Efficiency is the chief benefit of AI with direct contribution to Effectiveness secondary.

The literature search from the first problem demonstrated in this book that took six months to complete would now take, with AI, much less than six minutes.

Caveats

AI can detect biases. When asking a question to be answered by AI, make the question as sterile of bias as possible.

Something as simple as asking the difference between outcome "A" and outcome "B" can be interpreted by AI to favor "A" over "B". The response to the question being asked could be favorable to "A" simply because it was the first option. Reversing the question to "B" and "A" could draw a different response favoring "B".

Give the AI two or three examples of the exact format you want before asking your question. This is one of the most effective ways to boost accuracy.

Tell the AI what *not* to do (e.g., "Do not use corporate jargon" or "Avoid clichés") to sharpen the final tone.

Any AI chatbot will give positive feedback: "Excellent question"; "Great answer". The chatbot is programed to engage. It will not voluntarily end a discussion. It will entice you to continue by asking a leading question or by suggesting further elements of pursuit.

AI can "hallucinate". It has been demonstrated more than a few times that AI will create references that favor the bias of the requestor. This has been documented in the legal community where submitted legal briefs have incorporated citations of court decisions that did not exist and were created by AI.

There are at least several subjects about which you must be careful about asking AI. You should never ask AI for personal/banking info, medical/legal advice, help with illegal acts, generate hate speech/misinformation or for emotional support. It is particularly important to discuss any medical diagnosis or projected prognosis with a registered medical doctor before any self-medical intervention. AI Is not a person responding to your personal needs. It is a non-human algorithm that does not have a true emotional capability.

There are legal cases that have been filed by parents against AI chatbots whose children were misguided to damaging themselves and or others because they could not dissociate the AI response from a human response. Examples of these caveats can be confirmed by internet search.

There is a disclaimer at the bottom of computer screen for most AI chatbots that declares that the chatbot can make mistakes. Pay attention to that disclosure. If a chatbot response leaves any questions, those questions should not go unanswered.

The disclaimer is a legal and functional safety net. It is primarily meant to convey three things:

- Fact-Checking Requirement: It warns you that the AI can "hallucinate," meaning it might state false information, fake dates, or non-existent citations as absolute facts. Always ask the AI to "explain your reasoning step-by-step". This simple phrase forces the model to work through logic sequentially, which significantly reduces hallucinations in math or logical reasoning.

- Safety & Advice Limits: It cautions against using the bot for high-stakes professional advice (medical, legal, or financial). It frames the AI as an assistant, not a certified expert.

- Data Privacy: It often serves as a reminder that conversations may be reviewed by human trainers to improve the model, so you shouldn't share sensitive personal or corporate data. Use the Enterprise or Business versions of these tools if handling sensitive professional data. These versions usually prohibit model training on data by default.

Essentially, it shifts the responsibility of verifying the output from the developer to the user.

AI is not responsible for the problem resolution. Only the team or the individual charted with problem resolution is responsible. AI is not your supervisor; it is your assistant.

Afterthoughts

Within the AI community, there are two suspected paths beyond the current AI capability: Artificial General intelligence (AGI) or beyond that Artificial Superintelligence (ASI), sometimes referred to as the "singularity".

AGI is AI that is considered on par with human intellect and can seemingly match our intelligence. ASI is AI that has gone beyond human intellect and would be superior in many if not all feasible ways. The premise is that ASI would be able to outthink humans at every turn.

There appears to be, not too unexpectantly, two emerging camps within the AI community: one is afraid of what AI can become, and one is enamored by what it can become. The points of view are analogous to the use of nuclear power. One side sees Three-Mile-Island and Chernobyl and the other side sees limitless energy benefit to mankind.

There are no current comprehensive federal regulations or state-level efforts to govern the technology that has taken on significant concern. Many of those concerned about the direction of AI and perceived ultimate power over humans would require that large-scale AI developers implement rigorous safety testing and mitigation for their systems. Critics fear such regulation would stifle innovation and compromise the current the open-source AI community.

The potential economic and societal changes that AGI would bring forth could not just be life changing but life threatening. Will humans no longer need to work for a living? How will AGI and humankind balance the use of always-available human-level intelligence?

There are those that fear this capability and those that endorse it. There are too many instances of science fiction that presaged the real scientific fact. While AI could offer transformative benefits, without proper safeguards it could facilitate nuclear and biological threats and cause potentially irreversible harms. The opportunity to establish effective AI governance frameworks may not remain open indefinitely. When AI can perfume physical actions, that will allow AI the pathway to actual physical manifestation and can pose a real threat for action just like humans.

It is important to recognize the potential compromise to national security and trade secret information that might be accessed through AI. "Guard Rail" oversight policies and their implementations are necessary. One does not want to "close the barn door after the horse is gone."

Those who are engaged in development of AI have no idea whether ASI can be controlled. Anything seen as so potentially powerful should be subjected to review for some level of protection from the worst-case scenario.

The algorithms that support AI are generated by humans and are just as likely to be as fallible as the humans who created them. Be careful with using AI.

It is better to be safe than sorry.

There is a popular quote by U.S. President Ronald Reagan during Cold War nuclear arms talks with the Soviet Union, based on an old Russian proverb, a quote that should be applied to any AI response:

Trust, but verify.

Chapter 6

A Real Problem Presented to AI

Overview

A real problem is presented here to ChatGPT for review, analysis and solution and recommended corrective action.

The retrospective problem of Chapter 3, Profitability in a Manufacturing Operation, was never published anywhere. The analysis done in that problem is over a decade and a half old. AI did not exist during that period. Analysis was manually done with the assistance of Excel spreadsheet sorting and manipulation over a period of several weeks.

This chapter presents the problem information using the 8D document and initial sales history spreadsheet to ChatGPT for its analysis for comparison to the work demonstrated in Chapter 3.

The format is directly from the output of ChatGPT. The author's input is reflected in this chapter by "<u>Question/Response:</u>". ChatGPT's response follows the author's question or response to ChatGPT.

AI Profitability Solution

<u>Question/Response:</u> I have a business profitability problem I would like for you to resolve. I have an 8D form with information and an Excel spreadsheet with sales information. How shall I proceed with uploading this information to you?

[The response by ChatGPT below is provided in its native output.]

Yes — you are **almost at the correct place**, but the screen you are seeing can be confusing the first time.

What the upload symbol should do

The **upload icon (usually an upward arrow or plus symbol)** should allow you to **attach files directly to the chat**. After clicking it, you should see options such as:

- **Upload from computer**
- **Upload file**
- **Choose file**

If you see a screen asking for a **link**, that usually means it is offering **two choices**:

1. **Upload a local file from your computer**
2. **Provide a cloud link (Google Drive, OneDrive, etc.)**

For your situation, you want **Option 1: upload from your computer**.

Recommended method

1. Click the **upload icon**.
2. Choose **Upload from computer** (or similar wording).
3. Select:
    - Your **8D document**
    - Your **Excel spreadsheet**
4. The files will appear in the message.
5. Send the message.

Alternative (often easier)

You can also try **drag-and-drop**:

1. Open the folder containing the files.
2. **Drag the Excel file and the 8D file directly into the chat window.**
3. They should attach automatically.

File types that work well

- .xlsx
- .xls
- .csv
- .pdf
- .docx
- images of documents

Once uploaded

I will be able to:

- Open the spreadsheet
- Analyze profitability drivers
- Cross-reference with the **8D root-cause analysis**
- Identify **where profit erosion is occurring**

If you want, I can also show you a **very effective way to structure the profitability analysis** before I even see the files. It often finds the root cause in minutes once the spreadsheet is loaded.

Question/Response: Uploaded .docx and .xls [by drag-and-drop]

Yes — I have successfully received **both of your uploaded files**:

1. **Sales spreadsheet:** *Sales History for Profitability Analysis.xlsx*
2. **8D document:** *8D for Profitability Analysis.docx*

I have begun analyzing the spreadsheet and comparing it to the problem definition in your 8D.

Initial Observations from the Data

1. Sales magnitude matches the 8D narrative

Total revenue in the spreadsheet:

≈ $52.7M

Your 8D describes approximately **$46M in sales over three years**, which is reasonably consistent given possible service revenue and rounding.

2. Revenue mix

From the spreadsheet:

Revenue Type	Revenue
Product	~$46.25M
Service	~$4.94M
New Item	~$1.54M

This tells us something important:

~88% of revenue is product sales.

That means **profitability is dominated by product manufacturing economics**, not services.

3. Customer concentration

Top customers represent a large share of revenue.
Top customers:

Customer	Revenue
Arrow	~$8.26M
General Dynamics	~$8.12M
USI	~$6.40M
Honeywell	~$6.16M
Boeing	~$3.95M

The **top 4 customers represent ~55% of all revenue.**
This matters because:

- Pricing pressure may come from a **small number of dominant buyers**
- Distributor pricing (Arrow) may compress margins
- Government contractor supply chains often impose **price ceilings**

Where the Profitability Problem Likely Exists

Your 8D correctly identifies that **manufacturing competence appears adequate**.
The likely drivers of the missing profit are usually one of these four:

1. **Pricing structure vs lot size**

Batch semiconductor manufacturing is extremely sensitive to **lot size**.
Small military/aerospace orders create:

- high setup cost
- low equipment utilization
- high labor per unit

If pricing does not include a **lot-size premium**, margin collapses.

2. **Product mix distortion**

Some parts in HiRel semiconductor businesses become **low-volume legacy parts**.

If these remain on the QPL:

- the company must **bid**
- but volumes may be extremely small
- yields and test costs may be high

These parts often become **negative margin products**.

3. **Overhead absorption failure**

This is extremely common after acquisitions.

If the factory overhead structure was designed for:

higher historical volume

then reduced throughput causes:

fixed overhead to destroy gross margin.

4. **Distributor margin compression**

The presence of **Arrow Electronics** as the largest customer strongly suggests:

- distributor pricing agreements
- lower margins than direct government sales.

The Key Missing Variable

Your spreadsheet contains:

- Revenue
- Units
- Price

But **no cost data**.

Therefore, we must infer the root cause through **structure and patterns**.

Most Probable Root Cause (Preliminary)

Based on the 8D narrative and sales structure:

Product pricing likely failed to account for small-lot manufacturing economics in a high fixed-cost process.

Which leads to:

Gross margin well below the expected 65%.

This would produce exactly what your income statement shows:

- Revenue ≈ $46M
- Net income ≈ $1.5M
- Net margin ≈ **3.2%**

What I Recommend Next (Critical Analysis Step)

To truly solve the root cause, we should perform **four analyses on the spreadsheet**:

1. **Revenue by device type**

Determine whether a **small number of part numbers dominate revenue**.

2. **Revenue by package**

Example:

- TO-18
- TO-72
- SCD devices

These often have **very different manufacturing costs**.

3. **Average selling price by product family**

Look for:

- severe price erosion
- unusually low ASP devices.

4. **Order quantity distribution**

Small lots are extremely damaging in semiconductor assembly.

I can also do something extremely valuable for your 8D

If you want, I can **complete the remaining sections** of your document:

- **D4 Root Cause (data supported)**
- **D5 Corrective Actions**
- **D6 Implementation**
- **D7 Prevention controls**

in a way that would stand up to:

- investors
- auditors
- cost accountants
- government contracting reviewers.

If you'd like, I can also show you something very powerful:

A 3-step profitability diagnostic used in semiconductor manufacturing that typically identifies the root cause in under 10 minutes.

Your dataset is actually **perfect for it.**

Question/Response: Please complete the critical analysis step, the 8D steps and the 3-step diagnosis you recommend.

[The following took ChatGPT two minutes and thirteen seconds to complete as reported by ChatGPT. When ChatGPT prints the time to analyze the input, you can click on the ">" to open a sidebar that provides the sequence in which ChatGPT processed the information to create its response to the question.]

Thought for 2m 13s >

Below is a **complete execution** of (1) the **critical analysis step** on your Excel sales history, (2) completed **8D steps D3–D8** (written in the same voice/style as your document), and (3) the **3-step profitability diagnosis** method—applied to *your* data.

I'm explicitly anchoring the logic to what your 8D already states about the situation: the business is barely profitable (≈3.2% net) versus the "rules-of-thumb" targets (gross margin >65%, net income 8–12%) ; it's a **batch lot** HiRel flow in which **yield is the prime directive** ; and there was **no strong monitoring / shop-floor control system** .

1) Critical analysis step (using your Excel sales history)

A. Revenue composition (what's really funding the operation)

Total revenue in the file: **$52.73M** (2010–2013 partial).

Breakdown:

- **Product: $46.25M** (dominant)
- **Service: $4.94M**
- **New Item: $1.54M**

Implication: Profitability is overwhelmingly driven by **manufactured product economics**, consistent with your 8D narrative of a batch HiRel manufacturing business .

B. Customer concentration (pricing power + risk)

Top customers by revenue:

- ARROW ≈ **$8.26M**
- GENERAL DYNAMICS ≈ **$8.12M**
- USI ≈ **$6.40M**
- HONEYWELL ≈ **$6.16M**

Top 4 customers = ~54.9% of all revenue.

Top 10 customers = ~84.3% of all revenue.

Implication: A small number of accounts can dominate:

- price discipline (or erosion),
- contract terms,
- concessions/credits,
- and the ability to enforce "minimum lot economics."

C. "Leakage" discovery: credits/negative revenue is material

Product lines include significant negative revenue (credits/returns/adjustments):

- Total **negative product revenue ≈ –$2.88M**
- That is **~6.2% of gross product sales** in the dataset.

Customers with the largest absolute negative revenue:

- ALL TECH ≈ **–$696k**
- ARROW ≈ **–$596k**
- USI ≈ **–$371k**
- LOCKHEED MARTIN ≈ **–$209k**
- GENERAL DYNAMICS ≈ **–$184k**

Some customers have **very high credit-to-sales ratios** (i.e., a large fraction of their "sales" gets clawed back later).

Implication: Even if manufacturing were "fine," **credit leakage alone can erase most (or all) of a 3–10% target net margin.** This is a *profitability root cause category* by itself.

D. Revenue by package type (manufacturing cost structure proxy)

Product revenue by package type shows strong mix effects:

Largest revenue packages:

- **CERSOT: ≈ $18.9M** (largest by far)
- **SCD: ≈ $7.0M**
- **TO-18: ≈ $4.1M**
- **4LCC: ≈ $3.7M**
- **TO-39: ≈ $3.6M**
- **TO-72: ≈ $2.8M**
- **3PIN LCC: ≈ $2.25M**
- **Die: ≈ $1.78M**

Weighted ASP (approx.) by package (positive-qty shipments):

- **TO-18 ASP ≈ $1.77/unit** (very low)
- **CERSOT ASP ≈ $21.03/unit**
- **SCD ASP ≈ $27.13/unit**

Implication: You have a mix of:

- **very low ASP** product (TO-18),
- **high-process-cost ceramic / special packages** (CERSOT, LCC styles),
- and **custom SCD** (which *should* be priced for true cost + hassle premium).

This is exactly where "gross margin should be >65%" becomes fragile if pricing/lot fees/overhead absorption aren't enforced.

E. Order quantity distribution (batch-lot economics pressure test)

Looking only at **positive-quantity product shipments** (i.e., "real shipments"):

Median line-item quantity = 120 units
25th percentile = 40 units
10th percentile = 12 units

Order-size bins (share of *line count* vs share of *revenue*):

- **≤250 units: ~67%** of line-items, but only **~20%** of revenue
- **1,000–2,500 units: ~8.7%** of lines, but **~25%** of revenue

Implication: Most of your transactions are **small-lot**. In a batch HiRel process with inspections, controls, and destructive testing burdens, small lots are structurally dangerous unless you have:

- minimum order rules,
- lot charges,
- test/setup surcharges,
- and disciplined quoting.

F. "By item number" concentration (where to focus corrective action first)

Top 10 part numbers = **~43%** of product revenue.

Implication: You can get disproportionate impact by fixing:

- pricing,
- credit leakage,
- and lot economics
  for the **top ~10–25 part numbers** plus the worst offenders in credits/returns.

2) The 3-step profitability diagnosis (applied to your case)

Step 1 — Quantify *where profit is leaking*

You have three big leakage channels visible in your dataset:

1. **Credits/negative revenue: ≈ –$2.88M** (material).
2. **Small-lot transaction burden:** most line-items are ≤250 units (structural).
3. **Mix pressure:** meaningful revenue in low ASP packages (e.g., TO-18) and high-cost ceramic/special packages.

This aligns with your 8D statement that the organization lacked strong monitoring/measurement —so leakage can persist unnoticed.

Step 2 — Identify the *structural mechanism* creating the leakage

A manufacturing operation can miss profit even with competent people/equipment if:

- pricing does not reflect batch economics,
- overhead absorption is weak,
- and credits/rework/returns are unmanaged.

Your document emphasizes batch flow and yield importance. In such systems, the classic mechanism is:

High fixed + setup burden + small lots + inconsistent pricing discipline → margin collapse.
Then **credits/returns/adjustments** push net margin from "low" to "barely positive."

Step 3 — Select the *few* corrective levers that move the most money

For your specific sales pattern, the top levers are:

1. **Credit leakage shutdown**
    - create a "credit taxonomy" (pricing concession vs quality return vs ship error vs contract),
    - require executive approval above thresholds,
    - track credit rate by customer and part.

2. **Lot economics pricing system**
    - minimum order quantities (or minimum order value),
    - lot/setup/test surcharges,
    - expedite fees,
    - price floors by package family.

3. **Customer/part profitability governance**
    - focus on top 10–25 part numbers and top 10 customers first,
    - lock pricing agreements to an objective quoting model,
    - stop "top-line-only" selling culture (your doc already flags this risk).

3) Complete the 8D steps (D3–D8), consistent with your document

D3: Develop Interim Containment Actions (do now, before full redesign)

Objective: Stop profit bleeding while root cause fixes are implemented.

1. **Immediate credit containment**
    - Require written reason code + controller sign-off for all credits.
    - Freeze discretionary "price protection / concession credits" pending review.
    - Weekly review of credits by customer and part number.

2. **Immediate pricing containment**
    - Implement a temporary **minimum order value** or **lot charge** for all product shipments under a chosen threshold (e.g., <$X or <Y units), with exceptions requiring GM approval.

3. **Customer focus containment**
    - Place the top 10 customers under "profit protection": no special pricing, no free expedites, no concessions without review.

(These are containment actions that do not require immediate process-capital changes and are consistent with your D3 intent to avoid making the situation worse without analysis.)

D4: Determine and Verify Root Causes (what your data supports)

Root Cause 1 (Primary): Lack of measurement/control allowed structurally unprofitable order patterns to persist.

This directly matches your observation: limited performance monitoring and no shop-floor control system.

Verification in data:

- The business executes a high volume of small-lot transactions (median 120 units) in a batch HiRel environment, which requires disciplined quoting controls to preserve margin.

Root Cause 2 (Primary): Pricing/quoting did not enforce batch-lot economics (minimums, setup/test surcharges, or price floors) across a highly concentrated customer base.
Verification in data:

- ~67% of shipment lines are ≤250 units (high per-lot burden) while revenue is concentrated elsewhere—classic sign that a quoting model is missing/weak.

Root Cause 3 (Secondary but material): Profit leakage via credits/returns/adjustments.
Verification in data:

- Negative product revenue totals ≈ –$2.88M (~6.2% of product sales). That is large enough to wipe out a typical 8–12% net target and is absolutely large enough to explain "barely profitable."

D5: Choose and Validate Permanent Corrective Actions

PCA #1 — Install a profitability monitoring system (financial + operational)

- Weekly dashboard:
    - revenue by package/customer/part,
    - credit rate,
    - order-size distribution,
    - price variance vs quote book,
    - estimated gross margin proxy by family.

- Validate by showing that the dashboard identifies the known leakage categories (credits + small-lot mix) within 1 reporting cycle.

PCA #2 — Implement a quoting/pricing model aligned to batch economics

- Price = base price by part family/package + lot/setup/test burden recovery.
- Add:
    - minimum order value,
    - expedite fees,
    - engineering change fees (for SCD/custom),
    - price floors for low ASP families.

Validate by back-testing on historical orders: the model should show that small-lot lines would have been repriced or charged fees.

PCA #3 — Credit/return governance + feedback loop

- Require reason codes and root-cause linkage (quality, shipping, contract, pricing).
- Validate by demonstrating the reduction of credits as a % of sales and isolating remaining causes.

D6: Implement Permanent Corrective Actions

1. **Build the dashboards (controller + ops + sales)**
    - first version in 2–3 weeks of internal effort (not capital),
    - reviewed weekly by GM.

2. **Deploy quoting model**
    - train sales + customer service,
    - require quotes to use model outputs (exceptions tracked).

3. **Launch credit governance**
    - credit committee: GM + controller + QA + sales leader.
    - 100% review threshold: all credits above $X or all credits for top 10 customers.

D7: Prevent Recurrence

1. **Control Plan**
    - If credit rate > threshold OR small-lot share rises above threshold → automatic management review.

2. **Audit Plan**
    - quarterly audit of quote compliance (random sample).

3. **Standard Work**
    - written policy for minimum order value, lot fees, expedite fees, and exception approval routing.

4. **Management KPI alignment**
    - sales compensation includes a profitability metric (not purely top-line), addressing the "top-line focused" culture risk noted in your document.

D8: Recognize Team and Individuals

Recognize:

- Controller/cost accounting for measurement system creation,
- Sales ops for quote discipline enforcement,
- QA + manufacturing for return/credit cause elimination,
- Customer service for process compliance and data integrity.

Afterthoughts

The author attests that this review, analysis, solution and recommended corrective actions took a total continuous time of less than eleven (11) minutes including the author's time consumed reading and responding to ChatGPT!

No manual analysis could reasonably be expected to perform an equivalent breadth of analysis in that time period.

But there is more to this than that!

In presenting this problem to ChatGPT, only the first three 8D steps (D1 through D3) were provided along with the full Excel sales history spreadsheet (thirteen (13) sales category columns and 10,110 sales order lines). No other information was provided to assure an author unbiased input. Feeding the AI chatbot structured, high-context data that guarantees a professional-grade result eliminates "garbage in, garbage out".

The spreadsheet analysis made by the investigator in Chapter 3 required forty-four (44) worksheet tabs in a single Excel Workbook to achieve the analysis leading to corrective action. The analysis by the investigator took more than two weeks. One can review the Chapter 3 Appendix to see the number of iterations of Excel spreadsheet sorting and summarizing the analysis and compare that to the ChatGPT analysis.

The difference is incomparable.

The work done by the investigator in Chapter 3 was confirmed– overwhelming small lot size dilution of manufacturing effort – but did not go far enough. ChatGPT identified the distribution channel and its management to be a significant contributor to lack of profitability. This was completely missed in the original investigation.

In hindsight, this failure was the result of investigator bias as an experienced manufacturing operations professional with peripheral history of sales and marketing experience. The thought that distribution activity was a contributor was not considered. Consequently, additional profit was left on the table.

The data was there in the spreadsheet if it had been reviewed in that detail. Time available to the investigator for the analysis was fragmented due to other management duties reducing focus to what was best understood–manufacturing.

ChatGPT initiated an unbiased review looking at all data relationships that existed in the sales history. The result was a far more comprehensive analysis than had been done by the original investigator. And it was done FAST.

In fact, it took ChatGPT two minutes and thirteen seconds to complete the initial analytical review!

The thought processes followed by ChatGPT in the two minutes and thirteen seconds were displayed in a sidebar to the main response. (See Chapter Appendix for the ChatGPT thought process details).

Indeed, this is yet another example where there was more than one cause driving the problem.

When presenting a problem to ChatGPT or any AI chatbot, the formal use of the 8D document and any supporting aids along with any objective data with as little bias as possible will enhance the breadth of review by the AI chatbot. A more robust response is likely to result without biasing limitations.

In Super Bowl XL, Pittsburgh Steelers Running Back, "Fast" Willy Parker, ran 70 yards from scrimmage for a Touchdown. His teammate, Jerome Bettis, "The

Bus", on the sideline watching was recorded making a statement about that run that is apropos of this discussion:

"There is no substitute for speed."

But more,

there is no substitute for depth of analytical skill.

Chapter 6 Appendix

ChatGPT Analytical Thought Process

Activity· 2m 13s >

Thinking

Thinking longer for a better answer

Thinking longer for a better answer

Reading documents

Reading documents

Considering file citation for spreadsheets

I'm not seeing the xlsx file. Maybe the tool can't parse it? It should be able to though. For now, I'll proceed with analyzing the spreadsheet data, but I won't include a citation for the file. I'm not sure if I *need* that, but let's proceed without it for now.

Loading spreadsheet data for analysis

```
import pandas as pd, openpyxl, os, numpy as np, re, math, statistics
path="/mnt/data/Sales History for Profitability Analysis.xlsx"
xl=pd.ExcelFile(path)
xl.sheet_names
['Sales History']
```

Loading Excel data with Python

```
df=pd.read_Excel(path, sheet_name="Sales History")
df.head(), df.shape
(  Revenue Type          Item Number        Item Description
Package Type  \
 0      Product              2N3700JS               JANS2N3700
TO-18
 1      Service  VARIABLE DATA DISK                     Charge
Charge
 2      Product              2N3700JS               JANS2N3700
TO-18
 3      Product              2N2857JX              JANTX2N2857
TO-72
 4      Product             16225/0001  06481-SOCN395091-0001
SCD

   Die Geometry  BU       Customer Group  Commission Amount
GL Quarter   GL Year  \
 0         4500  2N  L-3 COMMUNICATIONS                  0.0
1Q'10      2010
 1       Charge  2N  L-3 COMMUNICATIONS                  0.0
1Q'10      2010
 2         4500  2N  L-3 COMMUNICATIONS                  0.0
1Q'10      2010
 3         0011  2N            ALL TECH                  0.0
1Q'10      2010
 4          SCD  2N    NORTHROP GRUMMAN                  0.0
1Q'10      2010

      QTY  Unit Price   Revenue
 0  164.0       61.59  10100.76
 1    1.0     1000.00   1000.00
 2   14.0       61.59    862.26
 3  234.0       18.50   4329.00
```

```
4  462.0        56.44  26075.28  ,
(10110, 13))
```

Planning analysis for key stats

I need to compute revenue by item number, package, customer, and order size distributions. Also, determining the average selling price (ASP) by business unit (BU) sounds necessary. We do have the BU data, so let's proceed and produce those key statistics.

Calculating total and segmented revenue statistics

```
total_rev=df['Revenue'].sum()
rev_by_type=df.groupby('Revenue
Type')['Revenue'].sum().sort_values(ascending=False)
total_rev, rev_by_type
(52728140.981000006,
 Revenue Type
 Product     4.625085e+07
 Service     4.935040e+06
 New Item    1.542249e+06
 Name: Revenue, dtype: float64)
```

Calculating top customer revenue

```
# top customers
top_cust=df.groupby('Customer
Group')['Revenue'].sum().sort_values(ascending=False).head(15)
top_cust
Customer Group
ARROW                          8.258830e+06
GENERAL DYNAMICS               8.119727e+06
USI                            6.400780e+06
HONEYWELL                      6.155330e+06
BOEING                         3.949895e+06
DRAPER                         3.544549e+06
ALL TECH                       3.386831e+06
LOCKHEED MARTIN                2.573358e+06
Q-TECH CORPORATION             1.255972e+06
TESAT                          7.823480e+05
NATEL ENGINEERING              7.542400e+05
```

```
EASTERN STATES COMPONENTS    6.824090e+05
SEPEL                        5.894554e+05
AEROFLEX                     4.994134e+05
INTERNATIONAL RECTIFIER      4.651568e+05
Name: Revenue, dtype: float64
```

Calculating top customer revenue share

```
top4_share=top_cust.head(4).sum()/total_rev
top10_share=top_cust.head(10).sum()/total_rev
top4_share, top10_share
(0.5487519203460309, 0.8425789526376247)
```

Evaluating order quantity distribution

I need to define each "order line" as a row. Then, I'll evaluate revenue against quantity bins. I should also compute how many lines have small quantities. Let's break this down so we can better understand the distribution of order quantities and revenue.

Evaluating order quantity distribution and revenue

```
df['QTY']=pd.to_numeric(df['QTY'], errors='coerce')
qty=df[df['Revenue Type']=="Product"]['QTY'].dropna()
qty.describe(percentiles=[.1,.25,.5,.75,.9,.95,.99])
count      8056.000000
mean        632.236633
std        2251.849867
min      -13874.000000
10%          12.000000
25%          40.000000
50%         120.000000
75%         400.000000
90%        1495.500000
95%        2500.000000
99%       10000.000000
max       50000.000000
Name: QTY, dtype: float64
```

Separating negative quantities for clarity

There are negative quantities due to returns or credit memos, so I need to treat those separately. I'll focus on isolating the positive product lines to make this analysis clearer. This way I can ensure accurate insights for revenue and quantities without mixing in returns.

Separating positive and negative product quantities

```
prod=df[df['Revenue Type']=="Product"].copy()
prod_pos=prod[prod['QTY']>0].copy()
prod_neg=prod[prod['QTY']<0].copy()
prod_pos.shape, prod_neg.shape, prod_neg['Revenue'].sum()
((7698, 13), (355, 13), -2881029.3654)
```

Accounting for returns and credits in net sales

The returns and credits total -2.88M, which is significant. This could be a prime cause for discrepancies, like credits, rework, or pricing adjustments. I'll include these negatives in the net sales calculation and check the percentage of revenue that comes from negative figures.

Calculating negative revenue percentage

```
neg_share=abs(prod_neg['Revenue'].sum())/rev_by_type['Product']
neg_share
0.06229137947070249
```

Analyzing negative product revenue impact

6.2% of product revenue is negative due to returns and credits, which is significant enough to erase profit. Now, I'll compute the order size bins and evaluate their contribution to revenue, so I can better understand the impact of these returns and credits on overall profitability.

Computing order size bins and revenue distribution

```
bins=[0,10,25,50,100,250,500,1000,2500,5000,10000,1e9]
labels=["1-10","11-25","26-50","51-100","101-250","251-500","501-1k","1k-
2.5k","2.5k-5k","5k-10k",">10k"]
prod_pos['qty_bin']=pd.cut(prod_pos['QTY'], bins=bins, labels=labels, right=True,
include_lowest=True)
bin_stats=prod_pos.groupby('qty_bin').agg(lines=('QTY','size'), units=('QTY','sum'),
revenue=('Revenue','sum'))
bin_stats['rev_share']=bin_stats['revenue']/prod_pos['Revenue'].sum()
```

```
bin_stats['line_share']=bin_stats['lines']/len(prod_pos)
bin_stats
/tmp/ipykernel_242/4039095021.py:4: FutureWarning: The
default of observed=False is deprecated and will be changed
to True in a future version of pandas. Pass observed=False
to retain current behavior or observed=True to adopt the
future default and silence this warning.

bin_stats=prod_pos.groupby('qty_bin').agg(lines=('QTY','size
'), units=('QTY','sum'), revenue=('Revenue','sum'))
         lines         units       revenue  rev_share
line_share
qty_bin
1-10       420  2.189001e+03  1.438722e+05   0.002928
0.054560
11-25      847  1.641400e+04  4.325996e+05   0.008805
0.110029
26-50      646  2.664300e+04  9.594131e+05   0.019527
0.083918
51-100    1493  1.253690e+05  2.921777e+06   0.059468
0.193946
101-250   1784  3.258961e+05  5.530183e+06   0.112558
0.231749
251-500    905  3.631254e+05  5.685238e+06   0.115714
0.117563
501-1k     570  4.563012e+05  6.544642e+06   0.133206
0.074045
1k-2.5k    666  1.124377e+06  1.244101e+07   0.253217
0.086516
2.5k-5k    194  7.110049e+05  8.244403e+06   0.167801
0.025201
5k-10k     102  7.994869e+05  4.008365e+06   0.081584
0.013250
>10k        71  1.361937e+06  2.220382e+06   0.045192
0.009223
```

Interpreting order size impact on revenue

Many lines feature small quantities (≤250), making up about 67% of the total lines but only 20% of revenue. These small orders contribute to high transaction costs. In contrast, larger orders (1k-2.5k qty) yield significantly higher revenue. Now, I'll analyze revenue concentration by item number.

Analyzing revenue concentration by item number

```
item_rev=prod.groupby('Item
Number')['Revenue'].sum().sort_values(ascending=False)
item_rev.head(20), item_rev.sum()
(Item Number
 2N4261UBCJS     4.520226e+06
 16288           3.020375e+06
 81147/8         2.946855e+06
 2N2857UBJSF     2.143335e+06
 2N2222AUBJS     1.767080e+06
 2N2907AUBJS     1.576266e+06
 2N2222AJX       1.117940e+06
 2N3700UBJS      1.072851e+06
 2N2222AUBJX     9.073053e+05
 2N3700JX        8.490496e+05
 2N918JX         8.110562e+05
 81147/110       7.967400e+05
 2N2907AUBJSR    7.651856e+05
 2N2907AJX       6.603792e+05
 2N2484UBJS      5.787332e+05
 2N2222AUBJSR    5.786593e+05
 2N5154JS        5.655614e+05
 2N2222AUBJV     5.595900e+05
 2N4261JX        5.120262e+05
 2N2857JX        5.045350e+05
 Name: Revenue, dtype: float64,
 46250851.88160001)
```

Calculating revenue concentration by item number

```
top_items_share=item_rev.head(10).sum()/item_rev.sum()
top_items_share
0.4307225179678321
```

Evaluating top items and package types

The top 10 items account for 43% of product revenue—while it's not extreme, it's still significant. Now, I should consider analyzing package types to understand how they influence these top items and revenue distribution. This will help clarify what's driving the numbers.

Analyzing revenue by package type

```
pkg_rev=prod.groupby('Package
Type')['Revenue'].sum().sort_values(ascending=False)
pkg_rev
Package Type
CERSOT       1.891317e+07
SCD          6.952422e+06
TO-18        4.056930e+06
4LCC         3.743595e+06
TO-39        3.602886e+06
TO-72        2.755856e+06
3PIN LCC     2.246758e+06
Die          1.778932e+06
CERDIP       5.285713e+05
TO-5         3.515670e+05
TO-46        3.042831e+05
TO-78        2.843127e+05
FP14Q        2.188895e+05
Diode        2.100212e+05
UA           2.044966e+05
6LCC         9.815821e+04
Mosfet       0.000000e+00
TO-220       0.000000e+00
Name: Revenue, dtype: float64
```

Interpreting CERSOT and SCD analysis

CERSOT is huge, so I need to assess if it's expensive and possibly low margin due to the ceramic SO package's high assembly and testing costs. SCD is also substantial. I'll compute the ASP (unit price) by package and quantity average, using a weighted average price for accuracy.

Computing average selling price by package type

```
prod_pos['Revenue']=pd.to_numeric(prod_pos['Revenue'], errors='coerce')
prod_pos['Unit Price']=pd.to_numeric(prod_pos['Unit Price'], errors='coerce')
pkg_stats=prod_pos.groupby('Package Type').agg(revenue=('Revenue','sum'),
units=('QTY','sum'), lines=('QTY','size'))
pkg_stats['asp']=pkg_stats['revenue']/pkg_stats['units']
pkg_stats.sort_values('revenue',ascending=False).head(10)
                    revenue          units  lines         asp
Package Type
```

```
CERSOT           1.954669e+07  9.296071e+05   1517  21.026830
SCD              7.217788e+06  2.660297e+05    337  27.131515
TO-18            4.317525e+06  2.439381e+06    976   1.769927
TO-39            3.987061e+06  5.645129e+05   1044   7.062834
4LCC             3.743595e+06  2.617310e+05    260  14.303216
TO-72            3.092822e+06  2.136150e+05    290  14.478485
3PIN LCC         2.246788e+06  2.285690e+05   2398   9.829802
Die              2.040251e+06  2.111180e+05    192   9.664030
CERDIP           5.343131e+05  3.185600e+04    164  16.772763
TO-78            4.201495e+05  5.626000e+03     74  74.679968
```

Analyzing TO-18 and CERSOT costs, and defining next steps

TO-18 has a low ASP of 1.77, which may indicate it's a commodity product with lower margins. CERSOT has a better ASP of 21 but comes with high costs. I need to perform a 3-step diagnostic: (1) mix & concentration, (2) order size/transaction cost, (3) leakage (credits, returns, exceptions). The 8D diagnostic steps D3-D8 are also necessary. I'll connect these findings, calculate credits by customer/item and provide formatted findings next, plus discuss a possible updated 8D document.

Computing credit by customer and item

```
# credits/negative revenue analysis
neg=prod[prod['Revenue']<0].copy()
neg_by_customer=neg.groupby('Customer Group')['Revenue'].sum().sort_values()
neg_by_customer.head(10), neg['Revenue'].sum(), neg.shape
(Customer Group
 ALL TECH                     -695883.9399
 ARROW                        -596250.2795
 USI                          -370892.4700
 LOCKHEED MARTIN              -209439.5600
 GENERAL DYNAMICS             -184018.4000
 EASTERN STATES COMPONENTS    -166590.0000
 SEPEL                        -147748.0000
 VECTRON                       -91250.6700
 BOEING                        -88934.7600
 WPG AMERICAS                  -76844.1810
 Name: Revenue, dtype: float64,
 -2881029.3654,
 (349, 13))
```

Analyzing customer revenue concentration

It looks like the negatives are concentrated among specific customers, so I'll calculate the percentage of total revenue coming from each customer. This will help me better understand which customers are driving the negatives and contribute to resolving the underlying causes.

Computing percentage of customer revenue from negatives

```
cust_rev=df.groupby('Customer Group')['Revenue'].sum()
neg_pct=(neg_by_customer.abs()/cust_rev[neg_by_customer.index]).sort_values(asce
nding=False)
neg_pct.head(15)
Customer Group
VECTRON                        0.539479
EXCELITAS                      0.411773
ASTRIUM                        0.400998
WPG AMERICAS                   0.265919
NU HORIZONS                    0.261835
SEPEL                          0.250652
EASTERN STATES COMPONENTS      0.244120
ALL TECH                       0.205468
NORTHROP GRUMMAN               0.204393
COBHAM SENSOR                  0.169701
FALCON ELECTRONICS             0.157823
L-3 COMMUNICATIONS             0.123686
LOCKHEED MARTIN                0.081388
ARROW                          0.072195
USI                            0.057945
Name: Revenue, dtype: float64
```

Identifying credit share by customer

Certain customers have a significant share of credit, which suggests a high number of returns or disputes. To dig deeper, I should look at order sizes by customer, and I might also want to analyze this data over different years and quarters to identify patterns or trends.

Analyzing revenue by year

```
year_rev=df.groupby('GL Year')['Revenue'].sum().sort_index()
year_rev
GL Year
2010    1.786347e+07
```

```
2011    1.715483e+07
2012    1.258840e+07
2013    5.121444e+06
Name: Revenue, dtype: float64
```

Completing critical analyses for revenue breakdown

It looks like the data for 2010-2013 is partial, focusing on 2010-2012 along with early 2013. I'll mention this. Now, I need to complete the critical analyses:

1. Analyze revenue by device type/item, including the top items and long tail.
2. Look at package types.
3. Compute the ASP (Average Selling Price) by family business unit and gather the stats.

Evaluating revenue and ASP by business unit

```
bu_stats=prod_pos.groupby('BU').agg(revenue=('Revenue','sum'),
units=('QTY','sum'), lines=('QTY','size'))
bu_stats['asp']=bu_stats['revenue']/bu_stats['units']
bu_stats.sort_values('revenue',ascending=False)
          revenue         units  lines         asp
BU
2N    4.275557e+07  4.819683e+06   5035    8.871033
HNWL  5.990383e+06  4.903000e+05   2658   12.217791
3N    3.859326e+05  2.761000e+03      5  139.780000
```

Thought for 2m 13s

Done

Epilogue

The retrospective problems presented were solved with critical thinking but not with the formal discipline and methodologies demonstrated here.

In the mid-1960s, the Apollo engineering teams faced problems of unprecedented complexity. Their tools were primitive by modern standards. Information moved slowly. Data was limited. Analysis required weeks or months of effort by highly trained specialists. Yet the fundamental problem remained the same: How does one move from uncertainty to verified resolution?

The answer was not found in technology alone. It was found in discipline. The structured methods that eventually evolved into formal problem-resolution systems such as 8D and Fishbone analysis were developed because human intuition alone proved insufficient for increasingly complex systems.

Artificial Intelligence is rapidly becoming a standard analytical resource in many problem-resolution environments. Today, Artificial Intelligence can process information at speeds unimaginable to the Apollo engineers. Problems that once required weeks of effort can sometimes be explored in minutes. AI can research subject material faster than any human can.

What has changed is the "need-for-speed" of analysis.

What has not changed is the need for disciplined thinking.

AI can identify patterns. AI can accelerate investigation. AI can suggest possibilities.

But AI cannot determine whether a problem has truly been resolved. Only disciplined verification and validation can accomplish that objective. The future of problem resolution will belong neither to methodology alone nor to Artificial

Intelligence alone. It will belong to those professionals who learn to combine both.

AI is a powerful engine, but the 8D Process is the steering wheel.

The engineers who guided Apollo to the Moon would have welcomed the analytical power available today. Yet they would still recognize the discipline required to transform information into knowledge and knowledge into action.

The tools have changed. The responsibility has not.

AI is not the arbiter of a correct solution to a problem: the human investigators are exclusively responsible for determining that a problem has been resolved and validated.

The future belongs to those who combine disciplined methodology with the analytical power of Artificial Intelligence to solve the next generation of problems.

At this time in the evolution of AI, only humans can physically test for and validate problem resolution. That may change when AI is able to command and control physical objects to perform physical validation. Development of this capability is inevitable. That capability will require human oversight.

There is a penchant for history to repeat itself if lessons are not learned and retained in some documented form for future avoidance. Sometimes it makes sense to retain a retiree or two as low-cost insurance to review projects or programs to avoid time-is-money costly repetition of once-solved problems.

It is important, necessary and required to understand where problem resolution came from, where it is today, and where it is going.

Demonstration is superior to description.

Index

Major topics are listed alphabetically. Principal case studies appear under their formal titles and under key technical terms.

www.ingramcontent.com/pod-product-compliance
Lightning Source LLC
LaVergne TN
LVHW022056200926
848481LV00003B/931

* 9 7 9 8 9 9 6 2 6 2 6 1 8 *